Handbook of Selected Court Cases

Third Edition

Handbook of Selected Court Cases

Third Edition

Australia • Canada • Mexico • Singapore • Spain • United Kingdom • United States

© 2005 Thomson Wadsworth, a part of The Thomson Corporation. Thomson, the Star logo, and Wadsworth are trademarks used herein under license.

ALL RIGHTS RESERVED. No part of this work covered by the copyright hereon may be reproduced or used in any form or by any means—graphic, electronic, or mechanical, including photocopying, recording, taping, Web distribution, information storage and retrieval systems, or in any other manner—without the written permission of the publisher.

Printed in the United States of America
1 2 3 4 5 6 7 08 07 06 05 04

Printer: Thomson West

ISBN 0-495-00352-2

For more information about our products, contact us at:
Thomson Learning Academic Resource Center
1-800-423-0563

For permission to use material from this text or product, submit a request online at
http://www.thomsonrights.com.
Any additional questions about permissions can be submitted by email to **thomsonrights@thomson.com**.

Thomson Higher Education
10 Davis Drive
Belmont, CA 94002-3098
USA

Asia (including India)
Thomson Learning
5 Shenton Way
#01-01 UIC Building
Singapore 068808

Australia/New Zealand
Thomson Learning Australia
102 Dodds Street
Southbank, Victoria 3006
Australia

Canada
Thomson Nelson
1120 Birchmount Road
Toronto, Ontario M1K 5G4
Canada

UK/Europe/Middle East/Africa
Thomson Learning
High Holborn House
50–51 Bedford Road
London WC1R 4LR
United Kingdom

Latin America
Thomson Learning
Seneca, 53
Colonia Polanco
11560 Mexico
D.F. Mexico

Spain (including Portugal)
Thomson Paraninfo
Calle Magallanes, 25
28015 Madrid, Spain

Table of Contents

Preface vii

Adarand Constructors, Inc. v. Pena..1
Atkins v. Virginia 9
Austin v. Michigan Chamber of Commerce 15
Baker v. Carr 21
Brown v. Board of Education 27
Bush v. Gore 33
Clinton v. Jones 39
De Jonge v. Oregon 45
Everson v. Board of Education...49
Ford v. Wainwright...55
In re Gault 61
Gibbons v. Ogden..69
Gideon v. Wainwright 75
Gitlow v. New York 81
Grutter v. Bollinger...87
Loving v. Virginia 93
Mapp v. Ohio..97
Marbury v. Madison 101
McCulloch v. Maryland..107
Miller v. California 111
Miranda v. Arizona...115
New York Times v. United States..121
Plessy v. Ferguson 127
Powell v. Alabama..131
Printz v. United States 137
Regents of the University of California v. Bakke 143
Reynolds v. Sims 149

TABLE OF CONTENTS

Roe v. Wade..**155**
Romer v. Evans...**161**
Sale v. Haitian Centers Council, Inc...........................**167**
Smith v. Allwright..**175**
U.S. Term Limits, Inc. v. Thornton..............................**181**
United Automobile Workers v. Johnson Controls, Inc................**187**
United States v. Harriss..**193**
United States v. Nixon..**199**
**United States Civil Service Commission v.
    National Association of Letter Carriers**................**207**
United Steelworkers of America v. Weber..................**213**
Wesberry v. Sanders..**219**
Youngstown Sheet & Tube Co. v. Sawyer...................**223**
Zurcher v. Stanford Daily...**229**

Preface

This booklet contains original source material pulled from important Supreme Court decisions as reported by West Group's WESTLAW Division. In order to make these case excerpts more understandable, we have broken them up into five parts.

- **The Case Citation**—This full citation includes the date the case was argued before the Supreme Court and the date that the Supreme Court decided the case.

- **Introduction**—This introduction is in our words and simply gives you and your students a brief idea of what the case involves.

- **WESTLAW Summary**—This summary is taken directly from WESTLAW, the computerized case reporting service of West Group. Of course, much of the language here is quite "legalese," but it does give a flavor of how the legal community would summarize the case under study.

- **Case Excerpts**—These are the actual words of the court. They are preceded by the name of the justice who rendered the Supreme Court decision. Of course, these are excerpts only, for many of these cases are extremely long. Note that citations have been deleted from the case excerpts.

- **Decision**—The actual decision, in the words of the court, is presented.

viii PREFACE

To help you understand case citations and other aspects of these important Supreme Court cases, we present below a summary of relevant information about court cases.

Federal Court Decisions

Federal trial court decisions are published unofficially in West's *Federal Supplement* (F.Supp.), and opinions from the circuit courts of appeals are reported unofficially in West's *Federal Reporter* (F., F.2d, or F.3d, where 2d refers to Second Series and 3d refers to Third Series). Cases concerning federal bankruptcy law are published unofficially in West's *Bankruptcy Reporter* (Bankr.). Opinions from the United States Supreme Court are reported in the *United States Reports* (U.S.), West's *Supreme Court Reporter* (S.Ct.), the *Lawyers' Edition of the Supreme Court Reports* (L.Ed. or L.Ed.2d), and other publications.

The *United States Reports* is the official edition of all decisions of the United States Supreme Court for which there are written opinions. Published by the federal government, the series includes reports of Supreme Court cases dating from the August term of 1791 although originally many of the decisions were not reported in the early volumes.

West's *Supreme Court Reporter* is an unofficial edition dating from the Court's term in October 1882. Preceding each of its case reports are a summary of the case and *headnotes* (brief editorial statements of the law involved in the case, numbered to correspond to numbers in the report). The headnotes are also given classification numbers that serve to cross-reference each headnote to other headnotes on similar points throughout the National Reporter System and other West publications to facilitate research of all relevant cases on a given point.

The Lawyers Cooperative Publishing Company of Rochester, New York, publishes the *Lawyers' Edition of the Supreme Court Reports,* which is an unofficial edition of the entire series of the Supreme Court reports and contains many of the decisions not reported in the early official volumes. Also, among other editorial features, the *Lawyers' Edition,* in its second series, precedes the report of each case with a full summary, includes excerpts from briefs of counsel, and discusses in detail selected cases of special interest to the legal profession.

A Sample Case Citation

The first case in this handbook is *Austin v. Michigan Chamber of Commerce*. Its full case citation is:

Richard H. **AUSTIN**
v.
MICHIGAN CHAMBER OF COMMERCE
494 U.S. 652, 110 S.Ct. 1391, 108 L.Ed.2d 652.

In other words, it lists three separate parallel citations:

494 U.S. 652 means that this case can be found in volume 494 of the *United States Reports*, the official edition of the decisions of the United States Supreme Court. The case starts on page 652.

110 S.Ct. 1391 is the citation from West's *Supreme Court Reporter*. This case can be found in volume 110 starting on page 1391.

108 L.Ed.2d 652 is a citation for the Second Series of the *Lawyers' Edition of the Supreme Court Reports*. This case is found in volume 108 starting on page 652.

You will notice that there are blanks in certain Supreme Court citations, such as for the first case in this handbook. Those blanks indicate that as yet there is no official citation for this case.

CASE TITLES

In the title of a case, such as *Austin v. Michigan Chamber of Commerce,* the *v.* or *vs.* stands for versus, which means against. (This is also called the *style* of the case, or the names of the parties in the lawsuit.) In the trial court, Austin was the plaintiff—the person who filed the suit. Michigan Chamber of Commerce was the defendant. If the case is appealed, however, the appellate court will sometimes place the name of the party appealing the decision first, so that the case may be called *Michigan Chamber of Commerce v. Austin.* Because some appellate courts retain the trial court order of names, it is often impossible to distinguish the plaintiff from the defendant in the title of a reported appellate court decision. The researcher must carefully read the facts of each case in order to identify each party. Otherwise, the discussion by the appellate court will be difficult to understand.

TERMINOLOGY

The following terms and phrases are frequently encountered in court opinions and legal publications. Because it is important to understand what is meant by these terms and phrases, we define and discuss them here.

Decisions and Opinions Most decisions reached by reviewing, or appellate, courts are explained in writing. A decision, or opinion, contains the court's reasons for its decision, the rules of law that apply, and the judgment. There are four possible types of written opinions for any particular case decided by an appellate court. When all judges or justices unanimously agree on an opinion, the opinion is written for the entire court and can be deemed a **unanimous opinion.** When there is not a unanimous opinion, a **majority opinion** is written, outlining the views of the majority of the judges or justices deciding the case. Often a judge or justice who feels strongly about making or emphasizing a point that was not made or emphasized in the unanimous or majority opinion will write a **concurring opinion.** That means the judge or justice agrees (concurs) with the judgment given in the unanimous or majority opinion, but for different reasons. In other than unanimous opinions, a **dissenting opinion** is usually written by a judge or justice who does not agree with the majority. The dissenting opinion is important because it may form the basis of the arguments used years later in overruling the precedential majority opinion.

Judges and Justices The terms *judge* and *justice* are usually synonymous and represent two designations given to judges in various courts. All members of the United States Supreme Court, for example, are referred to as justices. And justice is the formal title usually given to judges of appellate courts although this is not always the case. In New York, a justice is a trial judge of the trial court (which is called the Supreme Court), and a member of the Court of Appeals (the state's highest court) is called a judge. The term *justice* is commonly abbreviated to J., and *justices* to JJ. A Supreme Court case might refer to Justice Kennedy as Kennedy, J., or to Chief Justice Rehnquist as Rehnquist, C.J.

Appellants and Appellees The **appellant** is the party who appeals a case to another court or jurisdiction from the court or jurisdiction in which the case was originally brought. Sometimes, an appellant who appeals from a judgment is referred to as the **petitioner.** The **appellee** is the party against whom the appeal is taken. Sometimes, an appellee is referred to as the **respondent.**

ADARAND CONSTRUCTORS, INC.
v.
Federico **PENA**, Secretary of Transportation, et al.
515 U.S. 200, 115 S.Ct. 2097, 132 L.Ed.2d 158.
Argued Jan. 17, 1995.
Decided June 12, 1995.

Introduction

A case challenging a government program under which general contractors on government projects receive financial incentives to hire as subcontractors businesses that are owned by socially and economically disadvantaged individuals. The Court, overruling an earlier precedent holding that such actions were subject to intermediate scrutiny by the court, held that any race-based classification by any government (federal, state, or local) is subject to strict judicial scrutiny. Under this standard, racial classifications are constitutional only if they are narrowly tailored measures that further compelling governmental interests.

WESTLAW Summary

Subcontractor that was not awarded guardrail portion of federal highway project brought action challenging constitutionality of federal program designed to provide highway contracts to disadvantaged business enterprises. The United States District Court for the District of Colorado, Jim R. Carrigan, J., granted summary judgment in favor of defendants, and subcontractor appealed. The Court of Appeals affirmed, and certiorari was granted. The Supreme Court, Justice O'Connor, held that: (1) subcontractor had standing to seek forward-looking declaratory and injunctive relief; (2) all racial classifications, imposed by whatever federal, state, or local governmental actor, must be analyzed by reviewing court under strict scrutiny, overruling *Metro Broadcasting;* and (3) remand was required to determine whether challenged program satisfied strict scrutiny.

Case Excerpts

Justice O'CONNOR announced the judgment of the Court * * *.

Petitioner Adarand Constructors, Inc., claims that the Federal Government's practice of giving general contractors on government projects a financial incentive to hire subcontractors controlled by "socially and economically disadvantaged individuals," and in particular, the Government's use of race-based presumptions in identifying such individuals, violates the equal protection component of the Fifth Amendment's Due Process Clause. The Court of Appeals rejected Adarand's claim. We conclude, however, that courts should analyze cases of this kind under a different standard of review than the one the Court of Appeals applied. We therefore vacate the Court of Appeals' judgment and remand the case for further proceedings.

In 1989, the Central Federal Lands Highway Division (CFLHD), which is part of the United States Department of Transportation (DOT), awarded the prime contract for a highway construction project in Colorado to Mountain Gravel & Construction Company. Mountain Gravel then solicited bids from subcontractors for the guardrail portion of the contract. Adarand, a Colorado-based highway construction company specializing in guardrail work, submitted the low bid. Gonzales Construction Company also submitted a bid.

The prime contract's terms provide that Mountain Gravel would receive additional compensation if it hired subcontractors certified as small businesses controlled by "socially and economically disadvantaged individuals." Gonzales is certified as such a business; Adarand is not. Mountain Gravel awarded the subcontract to Gonzales, despite Adarand's low bid, and Mountain Gravel's Chief Estimator has submitted an affidavit stating that Mountain Gravel would have accepted Adarand's bid, had it not been for the additional payment it received by hiring

Gonzales instead. Federal law requires that a subcontracting clause similar to the one used here must appear in most federal agency contracts, and it also requires the clause to state that "[t]he contractor shall presume that socially and economically disadvantaged individuals include Black Americans, Hispanic Americans, Native Americans, Asian Pacific Americans, and other minorities, or any other individual found to be disadvantaged by the [Small Business] Administration pursuant to section 8(a) of the Small Business Act." Adarand claims that the presumption set forth in that statute discriminates on the basis of race in violation of the Federal Government's Fifth Amendment obligation not to deny anyone equal protection of the laws.

These fairly straightforward facts implicate a complex scheme of federal statutes and regulations, to which we now turn. The Small Business Act, as amended (Act), declares it to be "the policy of the United States that small business concerns, [and] small business concerns owned and controlled by socially and economically disadvantaged individuals, ... shall have the maximum practicable opportunity to participate in the performance of contracts let by any Federal agency." The Act defines "socially disadvantaged individuals" as "those who have been subjected to racial or ethnic prejudice or cultural bias because of their identity as a member of a group without regard to their individual qualities," and it defines "economically disadvantaged individuals" as "those socially disadvantaged individuals whose ability to compete in the free enterprise system has been impaired due to diminished capital and credit opportunities as compared to others in the same business area who are not socially disadvantaged."

In furtherance of the policy stated in s 8(d)(1), the Act establishes "[t]he Government-wide goal for participation by small business concerns owned and controlled by socially and economically disadvantaged individuals" at "not less than 5 percent of the total value of all prime contract and subcontract awards for each fiscal year." It also requires the head of each Federal agency to set agency-specific goals for participation by businesses controlled by socially and economically disadvantaged individuals.

* * * *

Adarand's claim arises under the Fifth Amendment to the Constitution, which provides that "No person shall ... be deprived of life, liberty, or property, without due process of law." Although this Court has always understood that Clause to provide some measure of protection against arbitrary treatment by the Federal Government, it is not as explicit a guarantee of equal treatment as the Fourteenth Amendment, which provides that "No State shall ... deny to any person within its jurisdiction the equal protection of the laws" (emphasis added). Our cases have accorded varying degrees of significance to the difference in the language of those two Clauses. * * *

* * * *

[In *Richmond v. J. A. Croson Co.*], the Court * * * agreed that the Fourteenth Amendment requires strict scrutiny of all race-based action by state and local governments. But *Croson* of course had no occasion to declare what standard of review the Fifth Amendment requires for such action taken by the Federal Government. * * * On the other hand, the Court subsequently indicated that *Croson* had at least some bearing on federal race-based action when it vacated a decision upholding such action and remanded for further consideration in light of *Croson*. Thus, some uncertainty persisted with respect to the standard of review for federal racial classifications.

Despite lingering uncertainty in the details, however, the Court's cases through *Croson* had established three general propositions with respect to governmental racial classifications. First, skepticism: " '[a]ny preference based on racial or ethnic criteria must necessarily receive a most searching examination,' " Second, consistency: "the standard of review under the Equal Protection Clause is not dependent on the race of those burdened or benefited by a particular classification," And third, congruence: "[e]qual protection analysis in the Fifth Amendment area is the same as that under the Fourteenth Amendment," Taken together, these three propositions lead to the conclusion that any person, of whatever race, has the right to demand that any governmental actor subject to the Constitution justify any racial classification subjecting that person to unequal treatment under the strictest judicial scrutiny. * * *

A year later, however, the Court took a surprising turn. *Metro Broadcasting, Inc. v. FCC* involved a Fifth Amendment challenge to two race-based policies of the Federal Communications Commission. In *Metro Broadcasting*, the Court repudiated the long-held notion that "it would be unthinkable that the same Constitution would impose a lesser duty on the Federal Government" than it does on a State to afford equal protection of the laws. It did so by holding that "benign" federal racial classifications need only satisfy intermediate scrutiny, even though *Croson* had recently concluded that such classifications enacted by a State must satisfy strict scrutiny. "[B]enign" federal racial classifications, the Court said, "—even if those measures are not 'remedial' in the sense of being designed to compensate victims of past governmental or societal discrimination—are constitutionally permissible to the extent that they serve important governmental objectives within the power of Congress and are substantially related to achievement of those objectives." The Court did not explain how to tell whether a racial classification should be deemed "benign," other than to express "confiden[ce] that an 'examination of the legislative scheme and its history' will separate benign measures from other types of racial classifications."

* * * *

* * * By adopting intermediate scrutiny as the standard of review for congressionally mandated "benign" racial classifications, *Metro Broadcasting* departed from prior cases in two significant respects. First, it turned its back on *Croson's* explanation of why strict scrutiny of all governmental racial classifications is essential * * *.

Second, *Metro Broadcasting* squarely rejected one of the three propositions established by the Court's earlier equal protection cases, namely, congruence between the standards applicable to federal and state racial classifications, and in so doing also undermined the other two—skepticism of all racial classifications, and consistency of treatment irrespective of the race of the burdened or benefited group. * * * *Metro Broadcasting* was thus a significant departure from much of what had come before it.

The three propositions undermined by *Metro Broadcasting* all derive from the basic principle that the Fifth and Fourteenth Amendments to the Constitution protect persons, not groups. It follows from that principle that all governmental action based on race—a group classification long recognized as "in most circumstances irrelevant and therefore prohibited"—should be subjected to detailed judicial inquiry to ensure that the personal right to equal protection of the laws has not been infringed. These ideas have long been central to this Court's understanding of equal protection, and holding "benign" state and federal racial classifications to different standards does not square with them. "[A] free people whose institutions are founded upon the doctrine of equality" should tolerate no retreat from the principle that government may treat people differently because of their race only for the most compelling reasons. Accordingly, we hold today that all racial classifications, imposed by whatever federal, state, or local governmental actor, must be analyzed by a reviewing court under strict scrutiny. In other words, such classifications are constitutional only if they are narrowly tailored measures that further compelling governmental interests. To the extent that *Metro Broadcasting* is inconsistent with that holding, it is overruled.

* * * *

* * * [W]e wish to dispel the notion that strict scrutiny is "strict in theory, but fatal in fact." The unhappy persistence of both the practice and the lingering effects of racial discrimination against minority groups in this country is an unfortunate reality, and government is not disqualified from acting in response to it. * * * When race-based action is necessary to further a compelling interest, such action is within constitutional constraints if it satisfies the "narrow tailoring" test this Court has set out in previous cases.

Because our decision today alters the playing field in some important respects, we think it best to remand the case to the lower courts for further consideration in light of the principles we have announced. The Court of Appeals * * * analyzed the case in terms of intermediate scrutiny. It upheld the challenged statutes and regulations because it found them to be "narrowly tailored to achieve [their] significant governmental purpose of providing subcontracting opportunities for small disadvantaged business enterprises." The Court of Appeals did not decide the question whether the interests served by the use of subcontractor compensation clauses are properly described as "compelling." It also did not address the question of narrow tailoring in terms of our strict scrutiny cases, by asking, for example, whether there was "any consideration of the use of race-neutral means to increase minority business participation" in government contracting, or whether the program was appropriately limited such that it "will not last longer than the discriminatory effects it is designed to eliminate."

* * * The question [as to] whether any of the ways in which the Government uses subcontractor compensation clauses can survive strict scrutiny, and any relevance distinctions such as these may have to that question, should be addressed in the first instance by the lower courts.

Decision

[T]he judgment of the Court of Appeals is vacated, and the case is remanded for further proceedings consistent with this opinion.

Daryl Renard **ATKIN**S
v.
VIRGINIA
536 U.S. 304, 122 S.Ct. 2242, 153 L.Ed.2d 335
Argued Feb. 20, 2002.
Decided June 20, 2002.

Introduction

In 1989, the U.S. Supreme Court ruled that executing mentally retarded defendants did not violate the Constitution. Thirteen years later, the Court decided to revisit the issue, taking the case of Daryl Atkins, a "mildly mentally retarded" man who had been convicted of abduction, armed robbery, and capital murder by a Virginia jury and sentenced to death. In deciding whether to uphold its earlier conclusion, the Court focused on evidence that public attitudes toward the death penalty had shifted significantly over the intervening years, and ruled accordingly.

WESTLAW Summary

Defendant was convicted, in the Circuit Court, York County, N. Prentis Smiley, Jr., J., of capital murder and was sentenced to death. The Virginia Supreme Court affirmed the conviction and sentence. Certiorari was granted. The Supreme Court, Justice Stevens, held that executions of mentally retarded criminals were "cruel and unusual punishments" prohibited by Eighth Amendment.

Case Excerpts

Justice STEVENS announced the judgment of the Court * * *.

Petitioner, Daryl Renard Atkins, was convicted of abduction, armed robbery, and capital murder, and sentenced to death. At approximately midnight on August 16, 1996, Atkins and William Jones, armed with a semiautomatic handgun, abducted Eric Nesbitt, robbed him of the money on his person, drove him to an automated teller machine in his pickup truck where cameras recorded their withdrawal of additional cash, then took him to an isolated location where he was shot eight times and killed.* * *

In the penalty phase, the defense relied on one witness, Dr. Evan Nelson, a forensic psychologist who had evaluated Atkins before trial and concluded that he was "mildly mentally retarded." His conclusion was based on interviews with people who knew Atkins, a review of school and court records, and the administration of a standard intelligence test which indicated that Atkins had a full scale IQ of 59.***

The jury sentenced Atkins to death. . .*** The Supreme Court of Virginia affirmed the imposition of the death penalty. Atkins did not argue before the Virginia Supreme Court that his sentence was disproportionate to penalties imposed for similar crimes in Virginia, but he did contend "that he is mentally retarded and thus cannot be sentenced to death." The majority of the state court rejected this contention, relying on our holding in *Penry v. Lynaugh*. The court was "not willing to commute Atkins' sentence of death to life imprisonment merely because of his IQ score." Because of the gravity of the concerns expressed by the dissenters, and in light of the dramatic shift in the state legislative landscape that has occurred in the past 13 years, we granted certiorari to revisit the issue that we first addressed in the *Penry* case.* * *

The Eighth Amendment succinctly prohibits "[e]xcessive" sanctions. It provides: "Excessive bail shall not be required, nor excessive fines imposed, nor cruel and unusual punishments inflicted." In *Weems v. United States,* we held that a punishment of 12 years jailed in irons at hard and painful labor for the crime of falsifying records was excessive. We explained "that it is a precept of justice that punishment for crime should be graduated and proportioned to [the] offense." We have repeatedly applied this proportionality precept in later cases interpreting the Eighth Amendment.* * *

A claim that punishment is excessive is judged not by the standards that prevailed in 1685 when Lord Jeffreys presided over the

"Bloody Assizes" or when the Bill of Rights was adopted, but rather by those that currently prevail. As Chief Justice Warren explained in his opinion in *Trop v. Dulles,* "The basic concept underlying the Eighth Amendment is nothing less than the dignity of man.... The Amendment must draw its meaning from the evolving standards of decency that mark the progress of a maturing society."

Proportionality review under those evolving standards should be informed by " 'objective factors to the maximum possible extent.' " We have pinpointed that the "clearest and most reliable objective evidence of contemporary values is the legislation enacted by the country's legislatures."

* * * *

Responding to the national attention received by . . . our decision in *Penry,* state legislatures across the country began to address the issue. In 1990, Kentucky and Tennessee enacted statutes similar to those in Georgia and Maryland, as did New Mexico in 1991, and Arkansas, Colorado, Washington, Indiana, and Kansas in 1993 and 1994. In 1995, when New York reinstated its death penalty, it emulated the Federal Government by expressly exempting the mentally retarded. Nebraska followed suit in 1998. There appear to have been no similar enactments during the next two years, but in 2000 and 2001 six more States--South Dakota, Arizona, Connecticut, Florida, Missouri, and North Carolina--joined the procession. The Texas Legislature unanimously adopted a similar bill, and bills have passed at least one house in other States, including Virginia and Nevada.

It is not so much the number of these States that is significant, but the consistency of the direction of change. Given the well-known fact that anticrime legislation is far more popular than legislation providing protections for persons guilty of violent crime, the large number of States prohibiting the execution of mentally retarded persons (and the complete absence of States passing legislation reinstating the power to conduct such executions) provides powerful evidence that today our society views mentally retarded offenders as categorically less culpable than the average criminal. The evidence carries even greater force when it is noted that the legislatures that have addressed the issue have voted

overwhelmingly in favor of the prohibition. Moreover, even in those States that allow the execution of mentally retarded offenders, the practice is uncommon. Some States, for example New Hampshire and New Jersey, continue to authorize executions, but none have been carried out in decades. Thus there is little need to pursue legislation barring the execution of the mentally retarded in those States. And it appears that even among those States that regularly execute offenders and that have no prohibition with regard to the mentally retarded, only five have executed offenders possessing a known IQ less than 70 since we decided Penry. The practice, therefore, has become truly unusual, and it is fair to say that a national consensus has developed against it.
* * * *

This consensus unquestionably reflects widespread judgment about the relative culpability of mentally retarded offenders, and the relationship between mental retardation and the penological purposes served by the death penalty. Additionally, it suggests that some characteristics of mental retardation undermine the strength of the procedural protections that our capital jurisprudence steadfastly guards.* * * Mentally retarded persons frequently know the difference between right and wrong and are competent to stand trial. Because of their impairments, however, by definition they have diminished capacities to understand and process information, to communicate, to abstract from mistakes and learn from experience, to engage in logical reasoning, to control impulses, and to understand the reactions of others. There is no evidence that they are more likely to engage in criminal conduct than others, but there is abundant evidence that they often act on impulse rather than pursuant to a premeditated plan, and that in group settings they are followers rather than leaders. Their deficiencies do not warrant an exemption from criminal sanctions, but they do diminish their personal culpability.
* * * *

Our independent evaluation of the issue reveals no reason to disagree with the judgment of "the legislatures that have recently addressed the matter" and concluded that death is not a suitable punishment for a mentally retarded criminal. * * * Construing and applying the Eighth Amendment in the light of our "evolving standards of decency," we therefore conclude that such punishment is excessive and that the Constitution "places a substantive restriction on the State's power to take the life" of a mentally retarded offender.

Decision

The judgment of the Virginia Supreme Court is reversed and the case is remanded for further proceedings not inconsistent with this opinion.

Richard H. **AUSTIN**
v.
MICHIGAN CHAMBER OF COMMERCE
494 U.S. 652, 110 S.Ct. 1391, 108 L.Ed.2d 652.
Argued Oct. 31, 1989.
Decided March 27, 1990.

Introduction

A First Amendment/Fourteenth Amendment case involving corporate rights to freedom of expression in the form of political campaign contributions. The Supreme Court held that a Michigan statute prohibiting corporations from using general corporate funds in political campaigns was constitutional and did not violate the First or Fourteenth Amendments.

WESTLAW Summary

Business organization brought action challenging Michigan statute prohibiting corporations from using corporate treasury funds for independent expenditures in support of or in opposition to candidates in elections for state office. The United States District Court for the Eastern District of Michigan upheld the statute and organization appealed. The Court of Appeals for the Sixth Circuit reversed. The Supreme Court, Justice Marshall, held that: (1) unique state-conferred corporate structure which facilitates the amassing of large treasuries warrants the limit on independent expenditures; (2) act is sufficiently narrowly tailored to achieve its goal; (3) act may be constitutionally applied to not-for-profit corporations; (4) there is no equal protection violation in fact that act does not apply to labor unions or unincorporated associations; and (5) there is no equal protection violation in fact that news media corporations are exempted from the prohibition.

Case Excerpts

Justice MARSHALL delivered the opinion of the Court.

In this appeal, we must determine whether [Section] 54(1) of the Michigan Campaign Finance Act violates either the First of the Fourteenth Amendment to the Constitution. Section 54(1) prohibits corporations from using corporate treasury funds for independent expenditures in support of or in opposition to any candidate in elections for state office. Corporations are allowed, however, to make such expenditures from segregated funds used solely for political purposes. * * *
* * * *
The Michigan State Chamber of Commerce, a nonprofit Michigan corporation, challenges the constitutionality of this statutory scheme. * * *

In June 1985 Michigan scheduled a special election to fill a vacancy in the Michigan House of Representatives. Although the Chamber had established and funded a separate political fund, it sought to use its general treasury funds to place in a local newspaper an advertisement supporting a specific candidate. As the Act made such an expenditure punishable as a felony, the Chamber brought suit in District Court for injunctive relief against enforcement of the Act, arguing that the restriction on expenditures is unconstitutional under both the First and the Fourteenth Amendments.

The District Court upheld the statute. The Sixth Circuit reversed, reasoning that the expenditure restrictions, as applied to the Chamber, violated the First Amendment. * * *

To determine whether Michigan's restrictions on corporate political expenditures may constitutionally be applied to the Chamber, we must ascertain whether they burden the exercise of political speech and, if they do, whether they are narrowly tailored to serve a compelling state interest. Certainly, the use of funds to support a political candidate is "speech"; independent campaign expenditures constitute "political expression 'at the core of our electoral process and of the First Amendment freedoms.'" The mere fact that the Chamber is a corporation does not remove its speech from the ambit of the First Amendment.

* * * *

The State contends that the unique legal and economic characteristics of corporations necessitate some regulation of their political expenditures to avoid corruption or the appearance of corruption. State law grants corporations special advantages—such as limited liability, perpetual life, and favorable treatment of the accumulation and distribution of assets—that enhance their ability to attract capital and to deploy their resources in ways that maximize the return on their shareholders' investments. These state-created advantages not only allow corporations to play a dominant role in the nation's economy, but also permit them to use "resources amassed in the economic marketplace" to obtain "an unfair advantage in the political marketplace." * * * The availability of these resources may make a corporation a formidable political presence, even though the power of the corporation may be no reflection of the power of its ideas. We therefore have recognized that "the compelling governmental interest in preventing corruption support[s] the restriction of the influence of political war chests funneled through the corporate form."

The Chamber argues that this concern about corporate domination of the political process is insufficient to justify restrictions on independent expenditures. Although this Court has distinguished these expenditures from direct contributions in the context of federal laws regulating individual donors, it has also recognized that a legislature might demonstrate a danger of real or apparent corruption posed by such expenditures when made by corporations to influence candidate elections. * * * We emphasize that the mere fact that corporations may accumulate large amounts of wealth is not the justification for [Section] 54; rather, the unique state-conferred corporate structure that facilitates the amassing of large treasuries warrants the limit on independent expenditures. Corporate wealth can unfairly influence elections when it is deployed in the form of independent expenditures, just as it can when it assumes the guise of political contributions. We therefore hold that the State has articulated a sufficiently compelling rationale to support its restriction on independent expenditures by corporations.

We next turn to the question whether the Act is sufficiently narrowly tailored to achieve its goal. We find that the Act is precisely targeted to eliminate the distortion caused by corporate spending while also allowing corporations to express their political views. * * * [T]he Act does not impose an absolute ban on all forms of corporate political spending but permits corporations to make independent political expenditures through separate segregated funds. Because persons contributing to such funds understand that their money will be used solely for political purposes, the speech generated accurately reflects contributors' support for the corporation's political views.

* * * *

The Chamber contends that even if the Campaign Finance Act is constitutional with respect to for-profit corporations, it nonetheless cannot be applied to a nonprofit ideological corporation like a chamber of commerce. * * *

* * * *

* * * [M]ore than three-quarters of the Chamber's members are business corporations, whose political contributions and expenditures can constitutionally be regulated by the State. As we read the Act, a corporation's payments into the Chamber's general treasury would not be considered payments to influence an election, so they would not be "contributions" or "expenditures," and would not be subject to the Act's limitations. Business corporations therefore could circumvent the Act's restrictions by funneling money through the Chamber's general treasury. Because the Chamber accepts money from for-profit corporations, it could, absent application of [Section] 54(1), serve as a conduit for corporate political spending. In sum, the Chamber does not possess the features that would compel the State to exempt it from restrictions on independent political expenditures.

The Chamber also attacks [Section] 54(1) as under inclusive because it does not regulate the independent expenditures of unincorporated labor unions. Whereas unincorporated unions, and indeed individuals, may be able to amass large treasuries, they do so without the significant state-conferred advantages of the corporate structure; corporations are "by far the most prominent example of entities that enjoy legal advantages enhancing their ability to accumulate wealth." The desire to counterbalance those advantages unique to the corporate form is the State's compelling interest in this case; thus, excluding from the statute's coverage unincorporated entities that also have the capacity to accumulate wealth "does not undermine its justification for regulating corporations."

* * * *

Because we hold that [Section] 54(1) does not violate the First Amendment, we must address the Chamber's contention that the provision infringes its rights under the Fourteenth Amendment. The Chamber argues that the statute treats similarly situated entities unequally. Specifically, it contends that the State should also restrict the independent expenditures of unincorporated associations with the ability to accumulate large treasuries and of corporations engaged in the media business.

Because the right to engage in political expression is fundamental to our constitutional system, statutory classifications impinging upon that right must be narrowly tailored to serve a compelling governmental interest. We find that, even under such strict scrutiny, the statute's classifications pass muster under the Equal Protection Clause. * * *

Similarly, we find that the Act's exemption of media corporations from the expenditure restrictions does not render the statute unconstitutional. The "media exception" excludes from the definition of "expenditure" any "expenditure by a broadcasting station, newspaper, magazine, or other periodical or publication for any news story, commentary, or editorial in support of or opposition to a candidate for elective office . . . in the regular course of publication or broadcasting." * * *

A valid distinction * * * exists between corporations that are part of the media industry and other corporations that are not involved in the regular business of imparting news to the public. Although the press' unique societal role may not entitle the press to greater protection under the Constitution, it does provide a compelling reason for the State to exempt media corporations from the scope of political expenditure limitations. * * *

Decision

The Court reversed the decision of the Court of Appeals.

Charles W. **BAKER** et al.
v.
Joe C. **CARR** et al.
369 U.S. 186, 82 S.Ct. 691, 7 L.Ed.2d 663.
Reargued Oct. 9, 1961.
Decided March 26, 1962.

Introduction

A Fourteenth Amendment/apportionment case in which the Court ruled that state legislatures had to be apportioned to provide equal protection under the law.

WESTLAW Summary

Action under the civil rights statute, by qualified voters of certain counties of Tennessee for a declaration that a state apportionment statute was an unconstitutional deprivation of equal protection of the laws, for an injunction, and other relief. A three-judge District Court, for the Middle District of Tennessee, entered an order dismissing the complaint, and plaintiffs appealed. The Supreme Court, Mr. Justice Brennan, held that complaint containing allegations that a state statute effected an apportionment that deprived plaintiffs of equal protection of the laws in violation of the Fourteenth Amendment presented a justiciable constitutional cause of action, and the right asserted was within reach of judicial protection under the Fourteenth Amendment, and did not present a nonjusticiable political question.

Case Excerpts

Mr. Justice BRENNAN delivered the opinion of the Court.

This civil action was brought * * * to redress the alleged deprivation of federal constitutional rights. The complaint, alleging that by

means of a 1901 statute of Tennessee apportioning the members of the General Assembly among the State's 95 counties, "these plaintiffs and others similarly situated, are denied the equal protection of the laws accorded them by the Fourteenth Amendment to the Constitution of the United States by virtue of the debasement of their votes," was dismissed by a three-judge court convened * * * in the Middle District of Tennessee. The court held that it lacked jurisdiction of the subject matter and also that no claim was stated upon which relief could be granted. We noted probable jurisdiction of the appeal. We hold that the dismissal was error, and remand the cause to the District Court for trial and further proceedings consistent with this opinion.
* * * *
* * * Tennessee's standard for allocating legislative representation among her counties is the total number of qualified voters resident in the respective counties, subject only to minor qualifications. * * * In 1901 the General Assembly abandoned separate enumeration in favor of reliance upon the Federal Census and passed the Apportionment Act here in controversy. In the more than 60 years since that action, all proposals in both Houses of the General Assembly for reapportionment have failed to pass.
* * * Indeed, the complaint alleges that the 1901 statute, even as of the time of its passage, "made no apportionment of Representatives and Senators in accordance with the constitutional formula * * *, but instead arbitrarily and capriciously apportioned representatives in the Senate and House without reference * * * to any logical or reasonable formula whatever." * * * [The plaintiffs] seek a declaration that the 1901 statute is unconstitutional and an injunction restraining the appellees from acting to conduct any further elections under it.

JURISDICTION OF THE SUBJECT MATTER

The District Court was uncertain whether our cases withholding federal judicial relief rested upon a lack of federal jurisdiction or upon the inappropriateness of the subject matter for judicial consideration—what we have designated "nonjusticiability." The distinction between the two grounds is significant. In the instance of nonjusticiability, consideration of the cause is not wholly and immediately foreclosed; rather, the Court's inquiry necessarily proceeds to the point of deciding whether the duty asserted can be judicially identified and its breach judicially determined, and whether protection for the right asserted can be judicially molded. In the instance of lack of jurisdiction the cause either does not "arise under" the Federal Constitution, laws or treaties (or fall within one of the other enumerated categories of Art[icle] III, [Section] 2), or is not a "case or controversy" within the meaning of that section; or the cause is not one described by any jurisdictional statute. Our conclusion that this cause presents no nonjusticiable "political question" settles the only possible doubt that it is a case or controversy. Under the present heading of "Jurisdiction of the Subject Matter" we hold only that the matter set forth in the complaint does arise under the Constitution. * * *

STANDING
* * * *

These appellants seek relief in order to protect or vindicate an interest of their own, and of those similarly situated. Their constitutional claim is, in substance, that the 1901 statute constitutes arbitrary and capricious state action, offensive to the Fourteenth Amendment in its irrational disregard of the standard of apportionment prescribed by the State's Constitution or of any standard, effecting a gross disproportion of representation to voting population. The injury which appellants assert is that this classification disfavors the voters in the counties in which they reside, placing them in a position of constitutionally unjustifiable inequality vis-a-vis voters in irrationally favored counties. * * *

JUSTICIABILITY

We have said that "In determining whether a question falls within (the political question) category, the appropriateness under our system of government of attributing finality to the action of the political departments and also the lack of satisfactory criteria for a judicial determination are dominant considerations." The nonjusticiability of a political question is primarily a function of the separation of powers.

Much confusion results from the capacity of the "political question" label to obscure the need for case-by-case inquiry. Deciding whether a matter has in any measure been committed by the Constitution to another branch of government, or whether the action of that branch exceeds whatever authority has been committed, is itself a delicate exercise in constitutional interpretation, and is a responsibility of this Court as ultimate interpreter of the Constitution.

* * * *

It is apparent that several formulations which vary slightly according to the settings in which the questions arise may describe a political question, although each has one or more elements which identify it as essentially a function of the separation of powers. Prominent on the surface of any case held to involve a political question is found a textually demonstrable constitutional commitment of the issue to a coordinate political department; or a lack of judicially discoverable and manageable standards for resolving it; or the impossibility of deciding without an initial policy determination of a kind clearly for nonjudicial discretion; or the impossibility of a court's undertaking independent resolution without expressing lack of the respect due coordinate branches of government; or an unusual need for unquestioning adherence to a political decision already made; or the potentiality of embarrassment from multifarious pronouncements by various departments on one question.

Unless one of these formulations is inextricable from the case at bar, there should be no dismissal for non-justiciability on the ground of a political question's presence. The doctrine of which we treat is one of "political questions," not one of "political cases." The courts cannot reject as "no law suit" a bona fide controversy as to whether some action denominated "political" exceeds constitutional authority. The cases we have reviewed show the necessity for discriminating inquiry into the precise facts and posture of the particular case, and the impossibility of resolution by any semantic cataloguing.

* * * *

We conclude then that the nonjusticiability of claims resting on the Guaranty Clause which arises from their embodiment of questions that were thought "political," can have no bearing upon the justiciability of the equal protection claim presented in this case. Finally, we emphasize that it is the involvement in Guaranty Clause claims of the elements thought to define "political questions," and no other feature, which could render them nonjusticiable. Specifically, we have said that such claims are not held nonjusticiable because they touch matters of state governmental organization.

* * * *

We conclude that the complaint's allegations of a denial of equal protection present a justiciable constitutional cause of action upon which appellants are entitled to a trial and a decision. The right asserted is within the reach of judicial protection under the Fourteenth Amendment.

Decision

The judgment of the District Court is reversed and the cause is remanded for further proceedings consistent with this opinion.

BROWN et al.
v.
BOARD OF EDUCATION OF TOPEKA, SHAWNEE COUNTY, KAN., et al.
347 U.S. 483, 74 S.Ct. 686, 98 L.Ed. 873.
Reargued Dec. 7, 8, 9, 1953.
Decided May 17, 1954.

Introduction

A classic civil rights case in which separate schools for black and white children were held to violate the equal protection clause of the Fourth Amendment.

WESTLAW Summary

Class actions originating in the four states of Kansas, South Carolina, Virginia, and Delaware, by which minor Negro plaintiffs sought to obtain admission to public schools on a nonsegregated basis. On direct appeals by plaintiffs from adverse decisions in the United States District Courts, District of Kansas, Eastern District of South Carolina, and Eastern District of Virginia, and on grant of certiorari after decision favorable to plaintiffs in the Supreme Court of Delaware, the United States Supreme Court, Mr. Chief Justice Warren, held that segregation of children in public schools solely on the basis of race, even though the physical facilities and other tangible factors may be equal, deprives the children of the minority group of equal educational opportunities, in contravention of the Equal Protection Clause of the Fourteenth Amendment.

Case Excerpts

Mr. Chief Justice WARREN delivered the opinion of the Court.

These cases come to us from the States of Kansas, South Carolina, Virginia, and Delaware. They are premised on different facts and different local conditions, but a common legal question justifies their consideration together in this consolidated opinion.

In each of the cases, minors of the Negro race, through their legal representatives, seek the aid of the courts in obtaining admission to the public schools of their community on a nonsegregated basis. In each instance, they have been denied admission to schools attended by white children under laws requiring or permitting segregation according to race. This segregation was alleged to deprive the plaintiffs of the equal protection of the laws under the Fourteenth Amendment. In each of the cases other than the Delaware case, a three-judge federal district court denied relief to the plaintiffs on the so-called "separate but equal" doctrine announced by this Court in *Plessy v. Ferguson*. Under that doctrine, equality of treatment is accorded when the races are provided substantially equal facilities, even though these facilities be separate. In the Delaware case, the Supreme Court of Delaware adhered to that doctrine, but ordered that the plaintiffs be admitted to the white schools because of their superiority to the Negro schools.

The plaintiffs contend that segregated public schools are not "equal" and cannot be made "equal," and that hence they are deprived of the equal protection of the laws. Because of the obvious importance of the question presented, the Court took jurisdiction. Argument was heard in the 1952 Term, and reargument was heard this Term on certain questions propounded by the Court.

Reargument was largely devoted to the circumstances surrounding the adoption of the Fourteenth Amendment in 1868. It covered exhaustively consideration of the Amendment in Congress, ratification by the states, then existing practices in racial segregation, and the views of proponents and opponents of the Amendment. This discussion and our own investigation convince us that, although these sources cast some light, it is not enough to resolve the problem with which we are faced. At best, they are inconclusive. The most avid proponents of the post-War Amendments undoubtedly intended them to remove all legal distinctions among "all persons born or naturalized in the United States." Their opponents, just as certainly, were antagonistic to both the letter and the spirit of the Amendments and wished them to have the most limited effect. What others in Congress and the state legislatures had in mind cannot be determined with any degree of certainty.

An additional reason for the inconclusive nature of the Amendment's history, with respect to segregated schools, is the status of public education at that time. In the South, the movement toward free common schools, supported by general taxation, had not yet taken hold. Education of white children was largely in the hands of private groups. Education of Negroes was almost nonexistent, and practically all of the race were illiterate. In fact, any education of Negroes was forbidden by law in some states. * * * It is true that public school education at the time of the Amendment had advanced further in the North, but the effect of the Amendment on Northern States was generally ignored in the congressional debates. Even in the North, the conditions of public education did not approximate those existing today. The curriculum was usually rudimentary; ungraded schools were common in rural areas; the school term was but three months a year in many states; and compulsory school attendance was virtually unknown. As a consequence, it is not surprising that there should be so little in the history of the Fourteenth Amendment relating to its intended effect on public education.

* * * *

In approaching this problem, we cannot turn the clock back to 1868 when the Amendment was adopted, or even to 1896 when *Plessy v. Ferguson* was written. We must consider public education in the light of its full development and its present place in American life throughout the Nation. Only in this way can it be determined if segregation in public schools deprives these plaintiffs of the equal protection of the laws.

Today, education is perhaps the most important function of state and local governments. Compulsory school attendance laws and the great expenditures for education both demonstrate our recognition of the importance of education to our democratic society. It is required in the performance of our most basic public responsibilities, even service in the armed forces. It is the very foundation of good citizenship. Today it is a principal instrument in awakening the child to cultural values, in preparing him for later professional training, and in helping him to adjust normally to his environment. In these days, it is doubtful that any child may reasonably be expected to succeed in life if he is denied the opportunity of an education. Such an opportunity, where the state has undertaken to provide it, is a right which must be made available to all on equal terms.

We come then to the question presented: Does segregation of children in public schools solely on the basis of race, even though the physical facilities and other "tangible" factors may be equal, deprive the children of the minority group of equal educational opportunities? We believe that it does.

In *Sweatt v. Painter*, in finding that a segregated law school for Negroes could not provide them equal educational opportunities, this Court relied in large part on "those qualities which are incapable of objective measurement but which make for greatness in a law school." In *McLaurin v. Oklahoma State Regents*, the Court, in requiring that a Negro admitted to a white graduate school be treated like all other students, again resorted to intangible considerations: " * * * his ability to study, to engage in discussions and exchange views with other students, and, in general, to learn his profession." Such considerations apply with added force to children in grade and high schools. To separate them from others of similar age and qualifications solely because of their race generates a feeling of inferiority as to their status in the community that may affect their hearts and minds in a way unlikely ever to be undone. The effect of this separation on their educational opportunities was well stated by a finding in the Kansas case by a court which nevertheless felt compelled to rule against the Negro plaintiffs: "Segregation of white and colored children in public schools has a detrimental effect upon the colored children. The impact is greater when it has the sanction of the law; for the policy of separating the races is usually interpreted as denoting the inferiority of the negro group. A sense of inferiority affects the motivation of a child to learn. Segregation with the sanction of law, therefore, has a tendency to (retard) the educational and mental development of Negro children and to deprive them of some of the benefits they would receive in a racial(ly) integrated school system."

Whatever may have been the extent of psychological knowledge at the time of *Plessy v. Ferguson*, this finding is amply supported by modern authority. Any language in *Plessy v. Ferguson* contrary to this finding is rejected.

We conclude that in the field of public education the doctrine of "separate but equal" has no place. Separate educational facilities are inherently unequal. Therefore, we hold that the plaintiffs and others similarly situated for whom the actions have been brought are, by reason of the segregation complained of, deprived of the equal protection of the laws guaranteed by the Fourteenth Amendment. * * *

Because these are class actions, because of the wide applicability of this decision, and because of the great variety of local conditions, the formulation of decrees in these cases presents problems of considerable complexity. On reargument, the consideration of appropriate relief was necessarily subordinated to the primary question—the constitutionality of segregation in public education. We have now announced that such segregation is a denial of the equal protection of the laws. In order that we may have the full assistance of the parties in formulating decrees, the cases will be restored to the docket. * * *

Decision

Cases ordered restored to docket for further argument on question of appropriate decrees.

George W. **BUSH**, *et al.*
v.
Albert **GORE**, Jr., *et al.*
531 U.S. 98, 121 S.Ct. 525, 148 L.Ed.2d 388.
December 12, 2000.

Introduction

This case decided the 2000 presidential election between Texas Governor George W. Bush and Vice President Al Gore. The conflict began when Florida officials refused to name a winner because of the closeness of the vote; under state law, such circumstances required a recount. Governor Bush, who enjoyed a narrow lead in the initial tally, argued that such a step would violate federal election law and the U.S. Constitution. Vice President Gore, in contrast, contended that various steps taken by Florida courts would result in a constitutionally acceptable recount. Because of the closeness of the race in the electoral college, whichever candidate "won" Florida would win the election.

WESTLAW Summary

Democratic candidates for President and Vice President of the United States filed complaint contesting certification of state results in presidential election. The Circuit Court, Leon County, N. Sanders Sauls, J., entered judgment denying all relief, and candidates appealed. The District Court of Appeal certified the matter to the Florida Supreme Court. On review, the Florida Supreme Court ordered manual recounts of ballots on which machines had failed to detect vote for President. Republican candidates filed emergency application for stay of Florida Supreme Court's mandate. The United States Supreme Court granted application, treating it as petition for writ of certiorari, and granted certiorari. The Supreme Court held that: (1) manual recounts ordered by Florida Supreme Court, without specific standards to implement its order to discern "intent of the voter," did not satisfy minimum requirement for non-arbitrary treatment of voters necessary, under Equal Protection Clause, to secure fundamental right to vote for President, and (2) remand of case to Florida Supreme Court for it to order constitutionally proper contest would not be appropriate remedy.

Case Excerpts

Per Curiam * * *

On November 8, 2000, the day following the Presidential election, the Florida Division of Elections reported that petitioner Bush had received 2,909,135 votes, and respondent Gore had received 2,907,351 votes, a margin of 1,784 for Governor Bush. Because Governor Bush's margin of victory was less than "one-half of a percent ... of the votes cast," an automatic machine recount was conducted under § 102.141(4) of the election code, the results of which showed Governor Bush still winning the race but by a diminished margin. Vice President Gore then sought manual recounts in Volusia, Palm Beach, Broward, and Miami-Dade Counties, pursuant to Florida's election protest provisions. A dispute arose concerning the deadline for local county canvassing boards to submit their returns to the Secretary of State (Secretary). The Secretary declined to waive the November 14 deadline imposed by statute. The Florida Supreme Court, however, set the deadline at November 26. We granted certiorari and vacated the Florida Supreme Court's decision, finding considerable uncertainty as to the grounds on which it was based. On December 11, the Florida Supreme Court issued a decision on remand reinstating that date.

On November 26, the Florida Elections Canvassing Commission certified the results of the election and declared Governor Bush the winner of Florida's 25 electoral votes. On November 27, Vice President Gore, pursuant to Florida's contest provisions, filed a complaint in Leon County Circuit Court contesting the certification. * * * The Circuit Court denied relief, stating that Vice President Gore failed to meet his burden of proof. He appealed to the First District Court of Appeal, which certified the matter to the Florida Supreme Court.* * *

The [Florida] Supreme Court held that Vice President Gore had satisfied his burden of proof with respect to his challenge to Miami-Dade County's failure to tabulate, by manual count, 9,000 ballots on which the machines had failed to detect a vote for President ("undervotes"). Noting the closeness of the election, the court explained that "[o]n this record, there can be no question that there are legal votes within the 9,000 uncounted votes sufficient to place the results of this election in doubt." A "legal vote," as determined by the Supreme Court, is "one in which there is a 'clear indication of the intent of the voter.' " The court therefore ordered a hand recount of the 9,000 ballots in Miami-Dade County. * * *

The petition presents the following questions: whether the Florida Supreme Court established new standards for resolving Presidential election contests, thereby violating Art. II, § 1, cl. 2, of the United States Constitution and failing to comply with 3 U.S.C. § 5, and whether the use of standardless manual recounts violates the Equal Protection and Due Process Clauses. With respect to the equal protection question, we find a violation of the Equal Protection Clause.
* * * *

The individual citizen has no federal constitutional right to vote for electors for the President of the United States unless and until the state legislature chooses a statewide election as the means to implement its power to appoint members of the electoral college. * * * History [now, however, favors] the voter, and in each of the several States the citizens themselves vote for Presidential electors. When the state legislature vests the right to vote for President in its people, the right to vote as the legislature has prescribed is fundamental; and one source of its fundamental nature lies in the equal weight accorded to each vote and the equal dignity owed to each voter. The State, of course, after granting the franchise in the special context of Article II, can take back the power to appoint electors. The right to vote is protected in more than the initial allocation of the franchise. Equal protection applies as well to the manner of its exercise. Having once granted the right to vote on equal terms, the State may not, by later arbitrary and disparate treatment, value one person's vote over that of another. It must be remembered that "the right of suffrage can be denied by a debasement or dilution of the weight of a citizen's vote just as effectively as by wholly prohibiting the free exercise of the franchise."

There is no difference between the two sides of the present controversy on these basic propositions. Respondents say that the very purpose of vindicating the right to vote justifies the recount procedures now at issue. The question before us, however, is whether the recount procedures the Florida Supreme Court has adopted are consistent with its obligation to avoid arbitrary and disparate treatment of the members of its electorate.

Much of the controversy seems to revolve around ballot cards designed to be perforated by a stylus but which, either through error or deliberate omission, have not been perforated with sufficient precision for a machine to register the perforations. In some cases a piece of the card—a chad—is hanging, say, by two corners. In other cases there is no separation at all, just an indentation.

The Florida Supreme Court has ordered that the intent of the voter be discerned from such ballots. For purposes of resolving the equal protection challenge, it is not necessary to decide whether the Florida Supreme Court had the authority under the legislative scheme for resolving election disputes to define what a legal vote is and to mandate a manual recount implementing that definition. The recount mechanisms implemented in response to the decisions of the Florida Supreme Court do not satisfy the minimum requirement for nonarbitrary treatment of voters necessary to secure the fundamental right. Florida's basic command for the count of legally cast votes is to consider the "intent of the voter." This is unobjectionable as an abstract proposition and a starting principle. The problem inheres in the absence of specific standards to ensure its equal application. The formulation of uniform rules to determine intent based on these recurring circumstances is practicable and, we conclude, necessary.

The law does not refrain from searching for the intent of the actor in a multitude of circumstances; and in some cases the general command to ascertain intent is not susceptible to much further refinement. In this instance, however, the question is not whether to believe a witness but how to interpret the marks or holes or scratches on an inanimate object, a piece of cardboard or paper which, it is said, might not have registered as a vote during the machine count. The factfinder confronts a thing, not a person. The search for intent can be confined by specific rules designed to ensure uniform treatment.

The want of those rules here has led to unequal evaluation of ballots in various respects. As seems to have been acknowledged at oral argument, the standards for accepting or rejecting contested ballots might vary not only from county to county but indeed within a single county from one recount team to another.

* * * *

In addition, the recounts in these three counties were not limited to so-called undervotes but extended to all of the ballots. The distinction has real consequences. A manual recount of all ballots identifies not only those ballots which show no vote but also those which contain more than one, the so-called overvotes. Neither category will be counted by the machine. This is not a trivial concern. At oral argument, respondents estimated there are as many as 110,000 overvotes statewide. As a result, the citizen whose ballot was not read by a machine because he failed to vote for a candidate in a way readable by a machine may still have his vote counted in a manual recount; on the other hand, the citizen who marks two candidates in a way discernible by the machine will not have the same opportunity to have his vote count, even if a manual examination of the ballot would reveal the requisite indicia of intent. Furthermore, the citizen who marks two candidates, only one of which is discernible by the machine, will have his vote counted even though it should have been read as an invalid ballot.* * *

That brings the analysis to yet a further equal protection problem. The votes certified by the court included a partial total from one county, Miami-Dade. The Florida Supreme Court's decision thus gives no assurance that the recounts included in a final certification must be complete. Indeed, it is respondents' submission that it would be consistent with the rules of the recount procedures to include whatever partial counts are done by the time of final certification, and we interpret the Florida

Supreme Court's decision to permit this. * * * The press of time does not diminish the constitutional concern. A desire for speed is not a general excuse for ignoring equal protection guarantees.

In addition to these difficulties the actual process by which the votes were to be counted under the Florida Supreme Court's decision raises further concerns. That order did not specify who would recount the ballots. The county canvassing boards were forced to pull together ad hoc teams of judges from various Circuits who had no previous training in handling and interpreting ballots. Furthermore, while others were permitted to observe, they were prohibited from objecting during the recount.

The recount process, in its features here described, is inconsistent with the minimum procedures necessary to protect the fundamental right of each voter in the special instance of a statewide recount under the authority of a single state judicial officer.

* * * *

Upon due consideration of the difficulties identified to this point, it is obvious that the recount cannot be conducted in compliance with the requirements of equal protection and due process without substantial additional work. * * * Because it is evident that any recount seeking to meet the December 12 date will be unconstitutional for the reasons we have discussed, we reverse the judgment of the Supreme Court of Florida ordering a recount to proceed.

Seven Justices of the Court agree that there are constitutional problems with the recount ordered by the Florida Supreme Court that demand a remedy.

Decision

The judgment of the Supreme Court of Florida is reversed, and the case is remanded for further proceedings not inconsistent with this opinion.

William Jefferson **CLINTON**
v.
Paula Corbin **JONES**
520 U.S. 681, 117 S.Ct. 1636, 137 L.Ed.2d 945.
Argued Jan. 13, 1997.
Decided May 27, 1997.

Introduction

In this case, the United States Supreme Court held that the president is not immune during a term in office from civil damages litigation concerning events that occurred before the president took office.

WESTLAW Summary

Former state employee sued sitting President of the United States alleging that President made "abhorrent" sexual advances while he was Governor of the State of Arkansas, and that her rejection of those advances led to retaliatory punishment by her supervisors. The United States District Court for the Eastern District of Arkansas, Susan Webber Wright, J., denied President's motion to dismiss, but granted president temporary immunity until he left office. Thereafter, President filed motion for stay pending appeal of court's order denying President's motion to dismiss on ground of presidential immunity. The District Court granted motion. Employee appealed. The Eighth Circuit Court of Appeals, Bowman, Circuit Judge, affirmed in part, reversed in part, and dismissed in part. The President petitioned for certiorari. The Supreme Court granted petition, and per Justice Stevens, held that: (1) Constitution does not afford President temporary immunity, in all but the most exceptional circumstances, from civil damages litigation arising out of events that occurred before he took office; (2) doctrine of separation of powers does not require federal courts to stay all private actions against President until he leaves office; and (3) District Court abused its discretion in deferring trial until after President left office.

Case Excerpts

Justice STEVENS delivered the opinion of the Court.

* * * *

The principal rationale for affording certain public servants immunity from suits for money damages arising out of their official acts is inapplicable to unofficial conduct. In cases involving prosecutors, legislators, and judges we have repeatedly explained that the immunity serves the public interest in enabling such officials to perform their designated functions effectively without fear that a particular decision may give rise to personal liability. * * * That rationale provided the principal basis for our holding that a former President of the United States was "entitled to absolute immunity from damages liability predicated on his official acts" [in a previous case]. Our central concern was to avoid rendering the President "unduly cautious in the discharge of his official duties."

This reasoning provides no support for an immunity for unofficial conduct. As we explained in [that case], "the sphere of protected action must be related closely to the immunity's justifying purposes." Because of the President's broad responsibilities, we recognized in that case an immunity from damages claims arising out of official acts extending to the "outer perimeter of his authority." But we have never suggested that the President, or any other official, has an immunity that extends beyond the scope of any action taken in an official capacity.

Moreover, when defining the scope of an immunity for acts clearly taken within an official capacity, we have applied a functional approach. * * * As our opinions have made clear, immunities are grounded in "the nature of the function performed, not the identity of the actor who performed it."

Petitioner's [the president's] effort to construct an immunity from suit for unofficial acts grounded purely in the identity of his office is unsupported by precedent.

* * * *

Petitioner's strongest argument supporting his immunity claim is based on the text and structure of the Constitution. He does not contend that the occupant of the Office of the President is "above the law," in the sense that his conduct is entirely immune from judicial scrutiny. The President argues merely for a postponement of the judicial proceedings that will determine whether he violated any law. His argument is grounded in the character of the office that was created by Article II of the Constitution, and relies on separation of powers principles that have structured our constitutional arrangement since the founding.

As a starting premise, petitioner contends that he occupies a unique office with powers and responsibilities so vast and important that the public interest demands that he devote his undivided time and attention to his public duties. He submits that—given the nature of the office—the doctrine of separation of powers places limits on the authority of the Federal Judiciary to interfere with the Executive Branch that would be transgressed by allowing this action to proceed.

* * * *

Petitioner's predictive judgment finds little support in either history or the relatively narrow compass of the issues raised in this particular case. * * * [I]n the more than 200-year history of the Republic, only three sitting Presidents have been subjected to suits for their private actions. If the past is any indicator, it seems unlikely that a deluge of such litigation will ever engulf the Presidency. As for the case at hand, if properly managed by the District Court, it appears to us highly unlikely to occupy any substantial amount of petitioner's time.

Of greater significance, petitioner errs by presuming that interactions between the Judicial Branch and the Executive, even quite burdensome interactions, necessarily rise to the level of constitutionally forbidden impairment of the Executive's ability to perform its constitutionally mandated functions. * * * The fact that a federal court's exercise of its traditional Article III jurisdiction may significantly burden the time and attention of the Chief Executive is not sufficient to establish a violation of the Constitution. Two long-settled propositions, first announced by Chief Justice Marshall, support that conclusion.

First, we have long held that when the President takes official action, the Court has the authority to determine whether he has acted within the law. Perhaps the most dramatic example of such a case is our holding that President Truman exceeded his constitutional authority when he issued an order directing the Secretary of Commerce to take possession of and operate most of the Nation's steel mills in order to avert a national catastrophe. Despite the serious impact of that decision on the ability of the Executive Branch to accomplish its assigned mission, and the substantial time that the President must necessarily have devoted to the matter as a result of judicial involvement, we exercised our Article III jurisdiction to decide whether his official conduct conformed to the law. * * *

Second, it is also settled that the President is subject to judicial process in appropriate circumstances. Although Thomas Jefferson apparently thought otherwise, Chief Justice Marshall, when presiding in the treason trial of Aaron Burr, ruled that a subpoena duces tecum could be directed to the President. We unequivocally and emphatically endorsed Marshall's position when we held that President Nixon was obligated to comply with a subpoena commanding him to produce certain tape recordings of his conversations with his aides. As we explained, "neither the doctrine of separation of powers, nor the need for confidentiality of high-level communications, without more, can sustain an absolute, unqualified Presidential privilege of immunity from judicial process under all circumstances."

* * * *

In sum, it is settled law that the separation-of-powers doctrine does not bar every exercise of jurisdiction over the President of the United States. If the Judiciary may severely burden the Executive Branch by reviewing the legality of the President's official conduct, and if it may direct appropriate process to the President himself, it must follow that the federal courts have power to determine the legality of his unofficial conduct. The burden on the President's time and energy that is a mere by-product of such review surely cannot be considered as onerous as the direct burden imposed by judicial review and the occasional invalidation of his official actions. We therefore hold that the doctrine of separation of powers does not require federal courts to stay all private actions against the President until he leaves office.

* * * *

* * * [W]e are persuaded that it was an abuse of discretion for the District Court to defer the trial until after the President leaves office. Such a lengthy and categorical stay takes no account whatever of the respondent's [Jones's] interest in bringing the case to trial. The complaint was filed within the statutory limitations period—albeit near the end of that period—and delaying trial would increase the danger of prejudice resulting from the loss of evidence, including the inability of witnesses to recall specific facts, or the possible death of a party.

* * * *

If Congress deems it appropriate to afford the President stronger protection, it may respond with appropriate legislation. As petitioner notes in his brief, Congress has enacted more than one statute providing for the deferral of civil litigation to accommodate important public interests. If the Constitution embodied the rule that the President advocates, Congress, of course, could not repeal it. But our holding today raises no barrier to a statutory response to these concerns.

The Federal District Court has jurisdiction to decide this case. Like every other citizen who properly invokes that jurisdiction, respondent has a right to an orderly disposition of her claims.

Decision

The Court affirmed the decision of the Court of Appeals.

DE JONGE
v.
State of **OREGON**.
299 U.S. 353, 57 S.Ct. 255, 81 L.Ed. 278.
Argued Dec. 9, 1936.
Decided Jan. 4, 1937.

Introduction

A freedom of assembly case involving a man convicted for holding a public meeting that was sponsored by the Communist Party. The Court overturned his conviction, ruling that the Oregon law restricted too much the rights of free speech and assembly. This case put the right of assembly on equal footing with the rights of free speech and press.

WESTLAW Summary

Dirk De Jonge was convicted of violating the Criminal Syndicalism Law of Oregon. The conviction was affirmed by the Supreme Court of Oregon, and Dirk De Jonge appeals.

Case Excerpts

Mr. Chief Justice HUGHES delivered the opinion of the Court.

Appellant, Dirk De Jonge, was indicted in Multnomah County, Oregon, for violation of the Criminal Syndicalism Law of that State. The act * * * defines "criminal syndicalism" as "the doctrine which advocates crime, physical violence, sabotage, or any unlawful acts or methods as a means of accomplishing or effecting industrial or political change or revolution." With this preliminary definition the act proceeds to describe a number of offenses, embracing the teaching of criminal syndicalism, the printing or distribution of books, pamphlets, etc., advocating that doctrine, the organization of a society or assemblage which advocates it, and presiding at or assisting in conducting a meeting of such an organization, society or group. * * *

* * * The charge is that appellant assisted in the conduct of a meeting which was called under the auspices of the Communist Party, an organization advocating criminal syndicalism. The defense was that the meeting was public and orderly and was held for a lawful purpose; that, while it was held under the auspices of the Communist Party, neither criminal syndicalism nor any unlawful conduct was taught or advocated at the meeting either by appellant or by others. Appellant moved for a direction of acquittal, contending that the statute as applied to him, for merely assisting at a meeting called by the Communist Party at which nothing unlawful was done or advocated, violated the due process clause of the Fourteenth Amendment of the Constitution of the United States. This contention was overruled. Appellant was found guilty as charged and was sentenced to imprisonment for seven years. The judgment was affirmed by the Supreme Court of the State which considered the constitutional question and sustained the statute as thus applied. The case comes here on appeal.

* * * *

* * * The stipulation does not disclose any activity by the defendant as a basis for his prosecution other than his participation in the meeting in question. Nor does the stipulation show that the communist literature distributed at the meeting contained any advocacy of criminal syndicalism or of any unlawful conduct. It was admitted by the Attorney General of the State in his argument at the bar of this Court that the literature distributed in the meeting was not of that sort and that the extracts contained in the stipulation were taken from communist literature found elsewhere. Its introduction in evidence was for the purpose of showing that the Communist Party as such did advocate the doctrine of criminal syndicalism, a fact which is not disputed on this appeal.

* * * *

In this view, lack of sufficient evidence as to illegal advocacy or action at the meeting became immaterial. Having limited the charge to defendant's participation in a meeting called by the Communist Party, the state court sustained the conviction upon that basis regardless of what was said or done at the meeting.

We must take the indictment as thus construed. Conviction upon a charge not made would be sheer denial of due process. It thus appears that, while defendant was a member of the Communist Party, he was not indicted for participating in its organization, or for joining it, or for soliciting members or for distributing its literature. He was not charged with teaching or advocating criminal syndicalism or sabotage or any unlawful acts, either at the meeting or elsewhere. He was accordingly deprived of the benefit of evidence as to the orderly and lawful conduct of the meeting and that it was not called or used for the advocacy of criminal syndicalism or sabotage or any unlawful action. His sole offense as charged, and for which he was convicted and sentenced to imprisonment for seven years, was that he had assisted in the conduct of a public meeting, albeit otherwise lawful, which was held under the auspices of the Communist Party.

* * * *

We are not called upon to review the findings of the state court as to the objectives of the Communist Party. Notwithstanding those objectives, the defendant still enjoyed his personal right of free speech and to take part in a peaceable assembly having a lawful purpose, although called by that party. The defendant was none the less entitled to discuss the public issues of the day and thus in a lawful manner, without incitement to violence or crime, to seek redress of alleged grievances. That was of the essence of his guaranteed personal liberty.

We hold that the Oregon statute as applied to the particular charge as defined by the state court is repugnant to the due process clause of the Fourteenth Amendment.

Decision

The judgment of conviction is reversed and the cause is remanded for further proceedings not inconsistent with this opinion.

EVERSON
v.
BOARD OF EDUCATION of Ewing TP. et al.
330 U.S. 1, 67 S.Ct. 504, 91 L.Ed. 711.
Argued Nov. 20, 1946.
Decided Feb. 10, 1947.
Rehearing Denied March 10, 1947.

Introduction

A First Amendment/establishment clause case in which the Court ruled in favor of tax-supported busing of students who attended parochial schools.

WESTLAW Summary

Certiorari proceedings by Arch R. Everson to set aside a resolution of the Board of Education of the Township of Ewing, in the County of Mercer, state of New Jersey, providing for the transportation of pupils to both public and parochial schools. A judgment setting aside the resolution was reversed by the Court of Errors and Appeals of New Jersey, and petitioner appeals.

Case Excerpts

Mr. Justice BLACK delivered the opinion of the Court.

A New Jersey statute authorizes its local school districts to make rules and contracts for the transportation of children to and from schools. The appellee, a township board of education, acting pursuant to this statute authorized reimbursement to parents of money expended by them for the bus transportation of their children on regular busses operated by the public transportation system. Part of this money was for the payment of transportation of some children in the community to Catholic parochial schools. These church schools give their students, in addition to secular education, regular religious instruction conforming to the religious tenets and modes of worship of the Catholic Faith. The superintendent of these schools is a Catholic priest.

The appellant, in his capacity as a district taxpayer, filed suit in a State court challenging the right of the Board to reimburse parents of parochial school students. He contended that the statute and the resolution passed pursuant to it violated both the State and the Federal Constitutions. That court held that the legislature was without power to authorize such payment under the State constitution. The New Jersey Court of Errors and Appeals reversed, holding that neither the statute nor the resolution passed pursuant to it was in conflict with the State constitution or the provisions of the Federal Constitution in issue. The case is here on appeal * * *.

* * * *

The only contention here is that the State statute and the resolution, in so far as they authorized reimbursement to parents of children attending parochial schools, violate the Federal Constitution in these two respects, which to some extent, overlap. They authorize the State to take by taxation the private property of some and bestow it upon others, to be used for their own private purposes. This, it is alleged violates the due process clause of the Fourteenth Amendment. The statute and the resolution forced inhabitants to pay taxes to help support and maintain schools which are dedicated to, and which regularly teach, the Catholic Faith. This is alleged to be a use of State power to support church schools contrary to the prohibition of the First Amendment which the Fourteenth Amendment made applicable to the states.

The due process argument that the State law taxes some people to help others carry out their private purposes is framed in two phases. The first phase is that a state cannot tax A to reimburse B for the cost of transporting his children to church schools. This is said to violate the due process clause because the children are sent to these church schools to satisfy the personal desires of their parents, rather than the public's interest in the general education of all children. This argument, if valid, would apply equally to prohibit state payment for the transportation of children to any non-public school, whether operated by a church, or any other nongovernment individual or group. But the New Jersey legislature has decided that a public purpose will be served by using tax-raised funds to pay the bus fares of all school children, including those who attend parochial schools. The New Jersey Court of Errors and Appeals has reached the same conclusion. The fact that a state law, passed to satisfy a public need, coincides with the personal desires of the individuals most directly affected is certainly an inadequate reason for us to say that a legislature has erroneously appraised the public need.

* * * *

Insofar as the second phase of the due process argument may differ from the first, it is by suggesting that taxation for transportation of children to church schools constitutes support of a religion by the State. But if the law is invalid for this reason, it is because it violates the First Amendment's prohibition against the establishment of religion by law. This is the exact question raised by appellant's second contention, to consideration of which we now turn.

The New Jersey statute is challenged as a "law respecting an establishment of religion." The First Amendment, as made applicable to the states by the Fourteenth, commands that a state "shall make no law respecting an establishment of religion, or prohibiting the free exercise thereof." These words of the First Amendment reflected in the minds of early Americans a vivid mental picture of conditions and practices which they fervently wished to stamp out in order to preserve liberty for themselves and for their posterity. Doubtless their goal has not been entirely reached; but so far has the Nation moved toward it that the expression "law respecting an establishment of religion," probably does not so vividly remind present-day Americans of the evils, fears, and political problems that caused that expression to be written into our Bill of Rights. Whether this New Jersey law is one respecting the "establishment of religion" requires an understanding of the meaning of that language, particularly with respect to the imposition of taxes. Once again, therefore, it is not inappropriate briefly to review the background and

environment of the period in which that constitutional language was fashioned and adopted.
    * * * *

The "establishment of religion" clause of the First Amendment means at least this: Neither a state nor the Federal Government can set up a church. Neither can pass laws which aid one religion, aid all religions, or prefer one religion over another. Neither can force nor influence a person to go to or to remain away from church against his will or force him to profess a belief or disbelief in any religion. No person can be punished for entertaining or professing religious beliefs or disbeliefs, for church attendance or non-attendance. No tax in any amount, large or small, can be levied to support any religious activities or institutions, whatever they may be called, or whatever from they may adopt to teach or practice religion. Neither a state nor the Federal Government can, openly or secretly, participate in the affairs of any religious organizations or groups and vice versa. * * *

We must consider the New Jersey statute in accordance with the foregoing limitations imposed by the First Amendment. But we must not strike that state statute down if it is within the state's constitutional power even though it approaches the verge of that power. New Jersey cannot consistently with the "establishment of religion" clause of the First Amendment contribute tax-raised funds to the support of an institution which teaches the tenets and faith of any church. On the other hand, other language of the amendment commands that New Jersey cannot hamper its citizens in the free exercise of their own religion. Consequently, it cannot exclude individual Catholics, Lutherans, Mohammedans, Baptists, Jews, Methodists, Non-believers, Presbyterians, or the members of any other faith, because of their faith, or lack of it, from receiving the benefits of public welfare legislation. While we do not mean to intimate that a state could not provide transportation only to children attending public schools, we must be careful, in protecting the citizens of New Jersey against state-established churches, to be sure that we do not inadvertently prohibit New Jersey from extending its general State law benefits to all its citizens without regard to their religious belief.

Measured by these standards, we cannot say that the First Amendment prohibits New Jersey from spending tax-raised funds to pay the bus fares of parochial school pupils as a part of a general program under which it pays the fares of pupils attending public and other schools. It is undoubtedly true that children are helped to get to church schools. There is even a possibility that some of the children might not be sent to the church schools if the parents were compelled to pay their children's bus fares out of their own pockets when transportation to a public school would have been paid for by the State. * * *

This Court has said that parents may, in the discharge of their duty under state compulsory education laws, send their children to a religious rather than a public school if the school meets the secular educational requirements which the state has power to impose. It appears that these parochial schools meet New Jersey's requirements. The State contributes no money to the schools. It does not support them. Its legislation, as applied, does no more than provide a general program to help parents get their children, regardless of their religion, safely and expeditiously to and from accredited schools.

The First Amendment has erected a wall between church and state. That wall must be kept high and impregnable. We could not approve the slightest breach. New Jersey has not breached it here.

Decision

Affirmed.

Alvin Bernard **FORD**, etc.
v.
Louie L. **WAINWRIGHT**
477 U.S. 399, 106 S.Ct. 2595, 91 L.Ed.2d 335.
Argued April 22, 1986.
Decided June 26, 1986.

Introduction

An Eighth Amendment/capital punishment case in which the Court ruled that the U.S. Constitution bars states from executing convicted killers who have become insane while waiting on death row.

WESTLAW Summary

A habeas corpus petition was filed on behalf of a death row prisoner. The United States District Court for the Southern District of Florida denied the petition, and appeal was taken. The United States Court of Appeals for the Eleventh Circuit, affirmed and denied rehearing, and the petitioner sought review. The Supreme Court, Justice Marshall held that: (1) Eighth Amendment prohibits state from inflicting the penalty of death upon a prisoner who is insane, and (2) Florida's procedures for determining sanity of a death row prisoner was not "adequate to afford a full and fair hearing" on the critical issue and therefore the habeas petitioner was entitled to an evidentiary hearing in the district court, de novo, on the question of his competence to be executed.

Case Excerpts

Justice MARSHALL announced the judgment of the Court.

For centuries no jurisdiction has countenanced the execution of the insane, yet this Court has never decided whether the Constitution forbids the practice. Today we keep faith with our common-law heritage in holding that it does.

Alvin Bernard Ford was convicted of murder in 1974 and sentenced to death. There is no suggestion that he was incompetent at the time of his offense, at trial, or at sentencing. In early 1982, however, Ford began to manifest gradual changes in behavior. They began as an occasional peculiar idea or confused perception, but became more serious over time. After reading in the newspaper that the Ku Klux Klan had held a rally in nearby Jacksonville, Florida, Ford developed an obsession focused upon the Klan. His letters to various people reveal endless brooding about his "Klan work," and an increasingly pervasive delusion that he had become the target of a complex conspiracy, involving the Klan and assorted others, designed to force him to commit suicide. He believed that the prison guards, part of the conspiracy, had been killing people and putting the bodies in the concrete enclosures used for beds. Later, he began to believe that his women relatives were being tortured and sexually abused somewhere in the prison. This notion developed into a delusion that the people who were tormenting him at the prison had taken members of Ford's family hostage. The hostage delusion took firm hold and expanded, until Ford was reporting that 135 of his friends and family were being held hostage in the prison, and that only he could help them. By "day 287" of the "hostage crisis," the list of hostages had expanded to include "senators, Senator Kennedy, and many other leaders." In a letter to the Attorney General of Florida, written in 1983, Ford appeared to assume authority for ending the "crisis," claiming to have fired a number of prison officials. He began to refer to himself as "Pope John Paul, III," and reported having appointed nine new justices to the Florida Supreme Court.

* * * *

Since this Court last had occasion to consider the infliction of the death penalty upon the insane, our interpretations of the Due Process Clause and the Eighth Amendment have evolved substantially. * * * Now that the Eighth Amendment has been recognized to affect significantly both the procedural and the substantive aspects of the death penalty, the question of executing the insane takes on a wholly different complexion. The adequacy of the procedures chosen by a State to determine sanity, therefore, will depend upon an issue that this Court has never addressed: whether the Constitution places a substantive restriction on the State's power to take the life of an insane prisoner.

* * * *

The Eighth Amendment prohibits the State from inflicting the penalty of death upon a prisoner who is insane. Petitioner's allegation of insanity in his habeas corpus petition, if proved, therefore, would bar his execution. The question before us is whether the District Court was under an obligation to hold an evidentiary hearing on the question of Ford's sanity. In answering that question, we bear in mind that, while the underlying social values encompassed by the Eighth Amendment are rooted in historical traditions, the manner in which our judicial system protects those values is purely a matter of contemporary law. Once a substantive right or restriction is recognized in the Constitution, therefore, its enforcement is in no way confined to the rudimentary process deemed adequate in ages past.

* * * *

Florida law directs the Governor, when informed that a person under sentence of death may be insane, to stay the execution and appoint a commission of three psychiatrists to examine the prisoner. * * * After receiving the report of the commission, the Governor must determine whether "the convicted person has the mental capacity to understand the nature of the death penalty and the reasons why it was imposed on him." If the Governor finds that the prisoner has that capacity, then a death warrant is issued; if not, then the prisoner is committed to a mental health facility. The procedure is conducted wholly within the executive branch, ex parte, and provides the exclusive means for determining sanity.

Petitioner received the statutory process. The Governor selected three psychiatrists, who together interviewed Ford for a total of 30 minutes, in the presence of eight other people, including Ford's counsel, the State's attorneys, and correctional officials. * * * That this most cursory form of procedural review fails to achieve even the minimal degree of reliability required for the protection of any constitutional interest * * * is self-evident.

The first deficiency in Florida's procedure lies in its failure to include the prisoner in the truth-seeking process. * * * [S]tate practice does not permit any material relevant to the ultimate decision to be submitted on behalf of the prisoner facing execution. In all other proceedings leading to the execution of an accused, we have said that the factfinder must "have before it all possible relevant information about the individual defendant whose fate it must determine." * * * It would be odd were we now to abandon our insistence upon unfettered presentation of relevant information, before the final fact antecedent to execution has been found.

Rather, consistent with the heightened concern for fairness and accuracy that has characterized our review of the process requisite to the taking of a human life, we believe that any procedure that precludes the prisoner or his counsel from presenting material relevant to his sanity or bars consideration of that material by the factfinder is necessarily inadequate. * * *

A related flaw in the Florida procedure is the denial of any opportunity to challenge or impeach the state-appointed psychiatrists' opinions. * * * Cross-examination of the psychiatrists, or perhaps a less formal equivalent, would contribute markedly to the process of seeking truth in sanity disputes by bringing to light the bases for each expert's beliefs, the precise factors underlying those beliefs, any history of error or caprice of the examiner, any personal bias with respect to the issue of capital punishment, the expert's degree of certainty about his or her own conclusions, and the precise meaning of ambiguous words used in the report. Without some questioning of the experts concerning their technical conclusions, a factfinder simply cannot be expected to evaluate the various opinions, particularly when they are themselves inconsistent. * * * The failure of the Florida procedure to afford the prisoner's representative any opportunity to clarify or challenge the state experts' opinions or methods creates a significant possibility that the ultimate decision made in reliance on those experts will be distorted.

Perhaps the most striking defect * * * is the State's placement of the decision wholly within the executive branch. Under this procedure, the person who appoints the experts and ultimately decides whether the State will be able to carry out the sentence that it has long sought is the Governor, whose subordinates have been responsible for initiating every stage of the prosecution of the condemned from arrest through sentencing. The commander of the State's corps of prosecutors cannot be said to have the neutrality that is necessary for reliability in the factfinding proceeding. * * *

Having identified various failings of the Florida scheme, we must conclude that the State's procedures for determining sanity are inadequate to preclude federal redetermination of the constitutional issue. We do not here suggest that only a full trial on the issue of sanity will suffice to protect the federal interests; we leave to the State the task of developing appropriate ways to enforce the constitutional restriction upon its execution of sentences. It may be that some high threshold showing on behalf of the prisoner will be found a necessary means to control the number of nonmeritorious or repetitive claims of insanity. * * *

* * * *

Decision

The judgment of the Court of Appeals is reversed, and the case remanded for further proceedings consistent with this opinion.

Application of Paul L. **GAULT** and Marjorie Gault, Father and Mother of Gerald
Francis Gault, a Minor
387 U.S. 1, 87 S.Ct. 1428, 18 L.Ed.2d 527.
Argued Dec. 6, 1966.
Decided May 15, 1967.

Introduction

A landmark case clarifying the constitutional and procedural rights of juveniles in juvenile court proceedings.

WESTLAW Summary

Proceeding on appeal from a judgment of the Supreme Court of Arizona, affirming dismissal of petition for writ of habeas corpus filed by parents to secure release of their 15-year-old son who had been committed as juvenile delinquent to state industrial school. The United States Supreme Court, Mr. Justice Fortas, held that juvenile has right to notice of charges, to counsel, to confrontation and cross-examination of witnesses, and to privilege against self-incrimination. Judgment reversed and cause remanded with directions.

Case Excerpts

Mr. Justice FORTAS delivered the opinion of the Court.

* * * *

On Monday, June 8, 1964, at about 10 a.m., Gerald Francis Gault and a friend, Ronald Lewis, were taken into custody by the Sheriff of Gila County. Gerald was then still subject to a six months' probation order which had been entered on February 25, 1964, as a result of his having been in the company of another boy who had stolen a wallet from a lady's purse. The police action on June 8 was taken as the result of a verbal complaint by a neighbor of the boys, Mrs. Cook, about a telephone call made to her in which the caller or callers made lewd or indecent remarks. * * *

At the time Gerald was picked up, his mother and father were both at work. No notice that Gerald was being taken into custody was left at the home. No other steps were taken to advise them that their son had, in effect, been arrested. Gerald was taken to the Children's Detention Home. * * *

On June 9, Gerald, his mother, his older brother, and Probation Officers Flagg and Henderson appeared before the Juvenile Judge in chambers. Gerald's father was not there. He was at work out of the city. Mrs. Cook, the complainant, was not there. No one was sworn at this hearing. No transcript or recording was made. No memorandum or record of the substance of the proceedings was prepared. * * * At the conclusion of the hearing, * * * Gerald was taken back to the Detention Home. * * *

* * * *

At [a] June 15 hearing a "referral report" made by the probation officers was filed with the court, although not disclosed to Gerald or his parents. This listed the charge as "Lewd Phone Calls." At the conclusion of the hearing, the judge committed Gerald as a juvenile delinquent to the State Industrial School "for the period of his minority (that is, until 21), unless sooner discharged by due process of law." * * *

No appeal is permitted by Arizona law in juvenile cases. On August 3, 1964, a petition for a writ of habeas corpus was filed with the Supreme Court of Arizona and referred by it to the Superior Court for hearing.

* * * *

The Superior Court dismissed the writ, and appellants sought review in the Arizona Supreme Court. That court stated that it considered appellants' assignments of error as urging (1) that the Juvenile Code is unconstitutional because it does not require that parents and children be apprised of the specific charges, does not require proper notice of a hearing, and does not provide for an appeal; and (2) that the proceedings and order relating to Gerald constituted a denial of due process of law because of the absence of adequate notice of the charge and the hearing; failure to notify appellants of certain constitutional rights including the rights to counsel and to confrontation, and the privilege against self-incrimination; the use of unsworn hearsay testimony; and the failure to make a record of the proceedings. Appellants further asserted that it was error for the Juvenile Court to remove Gerald from the custody of his parents without a showing and finding of their unsuitability, and alleged a miscellany of other errors under state law.

* * * *

The right of the state, as parents patriae, to deny to the child procedural rights available to his elders was elaborated by the assertion that a child, unlike an adult, has a right "not to liberty but to custody." He can be made to attorn to his parents, to go to school, etc. If his parents default in effectively performing their custodial functions—that is, if the child is "delinquent"—the state may intervene. In doing so, it does not deprive the child of any rights, because he has none. It merely provides the "custody" to which the child is entitled. On this basis, proceedings involving juveniles were described as "civil" not "criminal" and therefore not subject to the requirements which restrict the state when it seeks to deprive a person of his liberty.

* * * *

Accordingly, the highest motives and most enlightened impulses led to a peculiar system for juveniles, unknown to our law in any comparable context. The constitutional and theoretical basis for this peculiar system is—to say the least—debatable. And in practice, * * * the results have not been entirely satisfactory. Juvenile Court history has again demonstrated that unbridled discretion, however benevolently motivated, is frequently a poor substitute for principle and procedure. * * *

There is evidence * * * that there may be grounds for concern that the child receives the worst of both worlds: that he gets neither the protections accorded to adults nor the solicitous care and regenerative treatment postulated for children.

* * * *

Ultimately, however, we confront the reality of that portion of the Juvenile Court process with which we deal in this case. A boy is charged with misconduct. The boy is committed to an institution where he may be restrained of liberty for years. * * * Instead of mother and father and sisters and brothers and friends and classmates, his world is peopled by guards, custodians, state employees, and "delinquents" confined with him for anything from waywardness to rape and homicide.

In view of this, it would be extraordinary if our Constitution did not require the procedural regularity and the exercise of care implied in the phrase "due process." Under our Constitution, the condition of being a boy does not justify a kangaroo court. The traditional ideas of Juvenile Court procedure, indeed, contemplated that time would be available and care would be used to establish precisely what the juvenile did and why he did it—was it a prank of adolescence or a brutal act threatening serious consequences to himself or society unless corrected? Under traditional notions, one would assume that in a case like that of Gerald Gault, where the juvenile appears to have a home, a working mother and father, and an older brother, the Juvenile Judge would have made a careful inquiry and judgment as to the possibility that the boy could be disciplined and dealt with at home, despite his previous transgressions. Indeed, so far as appears in the record before us, except for some conversation with Gerald about his school work and his "wanting to go to * * * Grand Canyon with his father," the points to which the judge directed his attention were little different from those that would be involved in determining any charge of violation of a penal statute. The essential difference between Gerald's case and a normal criminal case is that safeguards available to adults were discarded in Gerald's case. The summary procedure as well as the long commitment was possible because Gerald was 15 years of age instead of over 18.

* * * *

NOTICE OF CHARGES

Appellants allege that the Arizona Juvenile Code is unconstitutional or alternatively that the proceedings before the Juvenile Court

were constitutionally defective because of failure to provide adequate notice of the hearings. * * *
   * * * *
   We cannot agree with [Supreme Court of Arizona's] conclusion that adequate notice was given in this case. Notice, to comply with due process requirements, must be given sufficiently in advance of scheduled court proceedings so that reasonable opportunity to prepare will be afforded, and it must "set forth the alleged misconduct with particularity." * * *

RIGHT TO COUNSEL
   Appellants charge that the Juvenile Court proceedings were fatally defective because the court did not advise Gerald or his parents of their right to counsel, and proceeded with the hearing, the adjudication of delinquency and the order of commitment in the absence of counsel for the child and his parents or an express waiver of the right thereto. The Supreme Court of Arizona * * * argued that "The parents and the probation officer may be relied upon to protect the infant's interests." Accordingly it rejected the proposition that "due process requires that an infant have a right to counsel." It said that juvenile courts have the discretion, but not the duty, to allow such representation * * * . We do not agree. * * * A proceeding where the issue is whether the child will be found to be "delinquent" and subjected to the loss of his liberty for years is comparable in seriousness to a felony prosecution. The juvenile needs the assistance of counsel to cope with problems of law, to make skilled inquiry into the facts, to insist upon regularity of the proceedings, and to ascertain whether he has a defense and to prepare and submit it. The child "requires the guiding hand of counsel at every step in the proceedings against him." * * *
   We conclude that the Due Process Clause of the Fourteenth Amendment requires that in respect of proceedings to determine delinquency which may result in the commitment to an institution in which the juvenile's freedom is curtailed, the child and his parents must be notified of the child's right to be represented by counsel retained by them,

or if they are unable to afford counsel, that counsel will be appointed to represent the child.
* * * *

CONFRONTATION, SELF-INCRIMINATION, CROSS-EXAMINATION

Appellants urge that the writ of habeas corpus should have been granted because of the denial of the rights of confrontation and cross-examination in the Juvenile Court hearings, and because the privilege against self-incrimination was not observed. * * *
* * * *

We shall assume that Gerald made admissions of the sort described by the Juvenile Court Judge * * * . Neither Gerald nor his parents were advised that he did not have to testify or make a statement, or that an incriminating statement might result in his commitment as a "delinquent."
* * * *

The privilege against self-incrimination is, of course, related to the question of the safeguards necessary to assure that admissions or confessions are reasonably trustworthy, that they are not the mere fruits of fear or coercion, but are reliable expressions of the truth. * * *

It would indeed be surprising if the privilege against self-incrimination were available to hardened criminals but not to children. The language of the Fifth Amendment, applicable to the States by operation of the Fourteenth Amendment, is unequivocal and without exception. And the scope of the privilege is comprehensive. * * *
* * * *

It is also urged, as the Supreme Court of Arizona here asserted, that the juvenile and presumably his parents should not be advised of the juvenile's right to silence because confession is good for the child as the commencement of the assumed therapy of the juvenile court process, and he should be encouraged to assume an attitude of trust and confidence toward the officials of the juvenile process. * * * In fact, evidence is accumulating that confessions by juveniles do not aid in "individualized treatment," as the court * * * put it, and that compelling the child to answer questions, without warning or advice as to his right to remain silent, does not serve this or any other good purpose. * * *

Decision

For the reasons stated, the judgment of the Supreme Court of Arizona is reversed and the cause remanded for further proceedings not inconsistent with this opinion.

Thomas **GIBBONS**
v.
Aaron **OGDEN**
22 U.S. 1, 9 Wheat. 1, 6 L.Ed.23.
Decided March 2, 1824.

Introduction

This was the first case presented to the United States Supreme Court under the commerce clause. In this case, the Court defined the scope of Congress's power to regulate interstate commerce, establishing the supremacy of the national government in all matters affecting interstate and foreign commerce.

Text Authors' Summary

Ogden operated steamboats in New York City under a monopoly granted by a statute passed by the New York state legislature. Gibbons operated competitive steamboats between New Jersey and New York under a federal license granted pursuant to a statute passed by Congress. Ogden filed a suit in the Court of Chancery of New York to obtain an injunction against Gibbons. Gibbons claimed that the New York law conflicted with the Constitution, which is the "Supreme Law of the Land." The New York court issued an injunction, which was upheld on Gibbons's appeal to the New York Court of Errors. Gibbons appealed to the United States Supreme Court. The Supreme Court dismissed Ogden's suit.

Case Excerpts

Mr. Chief Justice MARSHALL delivered the opinion of the Court.

* * * *

The words [in the Constitution] are, "Congress shall have power to regulate commerce with foreign nations, and among the several States, and with the Indian tribes."

The subject to be regulated is commerce; and our constitution being, as was aptly said at the bar, one of enumeration, and not of definition, to ascertain the extent of the power, it becomes necessary to settle the meaning of the word. The counsel for the appellee would limit it to traffic, to buying and selling, or the interchange of commodities, and do not admit that it comprehends navigation. This would restrict a general term, applicable to many objects, to one of its significations. Commerce, undoubtedly, is traffic, but it is something more: it is intercourse. It describes the commercial intercourse between nations, and parts of nations, in all its branches, and is regulated by prescribing rules for carrying on that intercourse. The mind can scarcely conceive a system for regulating commerce between nations, which shall exclude all laws concerning navigation, which shall be silent on the admission of the vessels of the one nation into the ports of the other, and be confined to prescribing rules for the conduct of individuals, in the actual employment of buying and selling, or of barter.
* * * *

The word used in the constitution, then, comprehends, and has been always understood to comprehend, navigation within its meaning; and a power to regulate navigation, is as expressly granted, as if that term had been added to the word "commerce."

To what commerce does this power extend? The constitution informs us, to commerce " * * * among the several States * * * ."
* * * *

* * * The word "among" means intermingled with. A thing which is among others, is intermingled with them. Commerce among the States, cannot stop at the external boundary line of each State, but may be introduced into the interior.

It is not intended to say that these words comprehend that commerce, which is completely internal, which is carried on between man and man in a State, or between different parts of the same State, and which does not extend to or affect other States. Such a power would be inconvenient, and is certainly unnecessary.

Comprehensive as the word "among" is, it may very properly be restricted to that commerce which concerns more States than one. * * *

The completely internal commerce of a State, then, may be considered as reserved for the State itself.

But, in regulating commerce with foreign nations, the power of Congress does not stop at the jurisdictional lines of the several States. It would be a very useless power, if it could not pass those lines. The commerce of the United States with foreign nations, is that of the whole United States. Every district has a right to participate in it. The deep streams which penetrate our country in every direction, pass through the interior of almost every State in the Union, and furnish the means of exercising this right. If Congress has the power to regulate it, that power must be exercised whenever the subject exists. If it exists within the States, if a foreign voyage may commence or terminate at a port within a State, then the power of Congress may be exercised within a State.

* * * *

We are now arrived at the inquiry—What is this power?

It is the power to regulate; that is, to prescribe the rule by which commerce is to be governed. This power, like all others vested in Congress, is complete in itself, may be exercised to its utmost extent, and acknowledges no limitations, other than are prescribed in the constitution. These are expressed in plain terms, and do not affect the questions which arise in this case, or which have been discussed at the bar. If, as has always been understood, the sovereignty of Congress, though limited to specified objects, is plenary as to those objects, the power over commerce with foreign nations, and among the several States, is vested in Congress as absolutely as it would be in a single government, having in its constitution the same restrictions on the exercise of the power as are found in the constitution of the United States. The wisdom and the discretion of Congress, their identity with the people, and the influence which their constituents possess at elections, are, in this, as in many other instances, as that, for example, of declaring war, the sole restraints on which they have relied, to secure them from its abuse. They are the restraints on which the people must often they solely, in all representative governments.

The power of Congress, then, comprehends navigation, within the limits of every State in the Union; so far as that navigation may be, in any manner, connected with "commerce with foreign nations, or among the several States, or with the Indian tribes." It may, of consequence, pass the jurisdictional line of New-York, and act upon the very waters to which the prohibition now under consideration applies.

But it has been urged with great earnestness, that, although the power of Congress to regulate commerce with foreign nations, and among the several States, be co-extensive with the subject itself, and have no other limits than are prescribed in the constitution, yet the States may severally exercise the same power, within their respective jurisdictions. In support of this argument, it is said, that they possessed it as an inseparable attribute of sovereignty, before the formation of the constitution, and still retain it, except so far as they have surrendered it by that instrument; that this principle results from the nature of the government, and is secured by the tenth amendment; that an affirmative grant of power is not exclusive, unless in its own nature it be such that the continued exercise of it by the former possessor is inconsistent with the grant, and that this is not of that description.

The appellant, conceding these postulates, except the last, contends, that full power to regulate a particular subject, implies the whole power, and leaves no residuum; that a grant of the whole is incompatible with the existence of a right in another to any part of it.

* * * *

Since, * * * in exercising the power of regulating their own purely internal affairs, whether of trading or police, the States may sometimes enact laws, the validity of which depends on their interfering with, and being contrary to, an act of Congress passed in pursuance of the constitution, the Court will enter upon the inquiry, whether the laws of New-York, as expounded by the highest tribunal of that State, have, in their application to this case, come into collision with an act of Congress, and deprived a citizen of a right to which that act entitles him. Should this collision exist, it will be immaterial whether those laws were passed in virtue of a concurrent power "to regulate commerce with foreign nations and among the several States," or, in virtue of a power to regulate their domestic trade and police. In one case and the other, the acts of New-York must yield to the law of Congress; and the decision sustaining the privilege they confer, against a right given by a law of the Union, must be erroneous.

* * * *

The questions, then, whether the conveyance of passengers be a part of the coasting trade, and whether a vessel can be protected in that occupation by a coasting license, are not, and cannot be, raised in this case. The real and sole question seems to be, whether a steam machine, in actual use, deprives a vessel of the privileges conferred by a license.

In considering this question, the first idea which presents itself, is, that the laws of Congress for the regulation of commerce, do not look to the principle by which vessels are moved. That subject is left entirely to individual discretion; and, in that vast and complex system of legislative enactment concerning it, which embraces every thing that the Legislature thought it necessary to notice, there is not, we believe, one word respecting the peculiar principle by which vessels are propelled through the water, except what may be found in a single act, granting a particular privilege to steam boats. With this exception, every act, either prescribing duties, or granting privileges, applies to every vessel, whether navigated by the instrumentality of wind or fire, of sails or machinery. The whole weight of proof, then, is thrown upon him who would introduce a distinction to which the words of the law give no countenance.

If a real difference could be admitted to exist between vessels carrying passengers and others, it has already been observed, that there is no fact in this case which can bring up that question. And, if the occupation of steam boats be a matter of such general notoriety, that the Court may be presumed to know it, although not specially informed by the record, then we deny that the transportation of passengers is their exclusive occupation. It is a matter of general history, that, in our western waters, their principal employment is the transportation of merchandise; and all know, that in the waters of the Atlantic they are frequently so employed.

But all inquiry into this subject seems to the Court to be put completely at rest, by the act already mentioned, entitled, "An act for the enrolling and licensing of steam boats."

This act authorizes a steam boat employed, or intended to be employed, only in a river or bay of the United States, owned wholly or in part by an alien, resident within the United States, to be enrolled and licensed as if the same belonged to a citizen of the United States.

This act demonstrates the opinion of Congress, that steam boats may be enrolled and licensed, in common with vessels using sails. They are, of course, entitled to the same privileges, and can no more be restrained from navigating waters, and entering ports which are free to such vessels, than if they were wafted on their voyage by the winds, instead of being propelled by the agency of fire. The one element may be as legitimately used as the other, for every commercial purpose authorized by the laws of the Union; and the act of a State inhibiting the use of either to any vessel having a license under the act of Congress, comes, we think, in direct collision with that act.

Decision

The Court reversed the decision of the New York court.

Clarence Earl **GIDEON**
v.
Louie L. **WAINWRIGHT**
372 U.S. 335, 83 S.Ct. 792, 9 L.Ed.2d 799.
Argued Jan. 15, 1963.
Decided March 18, 1963.

Introduction

A rights of the accused/right to counsel in which the Court said that persons who can demonstrate that they are unable to afford to have lawyer present and are accused of felonies must be given a lawyer at the expense of the government.

WESTLAW Summary

The petitioner brought habeas corpus proceedings against the Director of the Division of Corrections. The Florida Supreme Court denied all relief, and the petitioner brought certiorari. The United States Supreme Court held that the Sixth Amendment to the federal Constitution providing that in all criminal prosecutions the accused shall enjoy right to assistance of counsel for his defense is made obligatory on the states by the Fourteenth Amendment, and that an indigent defendant in a criminal prosecution in a state court has the right to have counsel appointed for him.

Case Excerpts

Mr. Justice BLACK delivered the opinion of the Court.

Petitioner was charged in a Florida state court with having broken and entered a poolroom with intent to commit a misdemeanor. This offense is a felony under Florida law. Appearing in court without funds and without a lawyer, petitioner asked the court to appoint counsel for him, whereupon the following colloquy took place:

"The COURT: Mr. Gideon, I am sorry, but I cannot appoint Counsel to represent you in this case. Under the laws of the State of Florida, the only time the Court can appoint Counsel to represent a Defendant is when that person is charged with a capital offense. I am sorry, but I will have to deny your request to appoint Counsel to defend you in this case."

"The DEFENDANT: The United States Supreme Court says I am entitled to be represented by Counsel."

Put to trial before a jury, Gideon conducted his defense about as well as could be expected from a layman. He made an opening statement to the jury, cross-examined the State's witnesses, presented witnesses in his own defense, declined to testify himself, and made a short argument "emphasizing his innocence to the charge contained in the Information filed in this case." The jury returned a verdict of guilty, and petitioner was sentenced to serve five years in the state prison. Later, petitioner filed in the Florida Supreme Court this habeas corpus petitioner attacking his conviction and sentence on the ground that the trial court's refusal to appoint counsel for him denied him rights "guaranteed by the Constitution and the Bill of Rights by the United States Government." Treating the petition for habeas corpus as properly before it, the State Supreme Court, "upon consideration thereof" but without an opinion, denied all relief. Since 1942, when *Betts v. Brady* was decided by a divided Court, the problem of a defendant's federal constitutional right to counsel in a state court has been a continuing source of controversy and litigation in both state and federal courts To give this problem another review here, we granted certiorari. Since Gideon was proceeding in forma pauperis, we appointed counsel to represent him and requested both sides to discuss in their briefs and oral arguments the following: "Should this Court's holding in *Betts v. Brady* be reconsidered?"

The facts upon which Betts claimed that he had been unconstitutionally denied the right to have counsel appointed to assist him are strikingly like the facts upon which Gideon here bases his federal constitutional claim. Betts was indicted for robbery in a Maryland state court. On arraignment, he told the trial judge of his lack of funds to hire a lawyer and asked the court to appoint one for him. Betts was advised that it was not the practice in that county to appoint counsel for indigent defendants except in murder and rape cases. He then pleaded not guilty, had witnesses summoned, cross-examined the State's witnesses, examined his own, and chose not to testify himself. He was found guilty by the judge, sitting without a jury, and sentenced to eight years in prison. Like Gideon, *Betts* sought release by habeas corpus, alleging that he had been denied the right to assistance of counsel in violation of the Fourteenth Amendment. *Betts* was denied any relief, and on review this Court affirmed. It was held that a refusal to appoint counsel for an indigent defendant charged with a felony did not necessarily violate the Due Process Clause of the Fourteenth Amendment, which for reasons given the Court deemed to be the only applicable federal constitutional provision. * * * Since the facts and circumstances of the two cases are so nearly indistinguishable, we think the *Betts v. Brady* holding if left standing would require us to reject Gideon's claim that the Constitution guarantees him the assistance of counsel. Upon full reconsideration we conclude that *Betts v. Brady* should be overruled.

    The Sixth Amendment provides, "In all criminal prosecutions, the accused shall enjoy the right * * * to have the Assistance of Counsel for his defense." We have construed this to mean that in federal courts counsel must be provided for defendants unable to employ counsel unless the right is competently and intelligently waived. Betts argued that this right is extended to indigent defendants in state courts by the Fourteenth Amendment. In response the Court stated that, while the Sixth Amendment laid down "no rule for the conduct of the states, the question recurs whether the constraint laid by the amendment upon the national courts expresses a rule so fundamental and essential to a fair trial, and so, to due process of law, that it is made obligatory upon the states by the Fourteenth Amendment." In order to decide whether the Sixth Amendment's guarantee of counsel is of this fundamental nature, the Court in Betts set out and considered "(r)elevant data on the subject * * * afforded by constitutional and statutory provisions subsisting in the colonies and the states prior to the inclusion of the Bill of Rights in the national Constitution, and in the constitutional, legislative, and judicial history of the states to the present date." On the basis of this historical data the Court concluded that "appointment of counsel is not a fundamental right, essential to a fair trial." * * *

* * * *

We accept *Betts v. Brady*'s assumption, based as it was on our prior cases, that a provision of the Bill of Rights which is "fundamental and essential to a fair trial" is made obligatory upon the States by the Fourteenth Amendment. We think the Court in Betts was wrong, however, in concluding that the Sixth Amendment's guarantee of counsel is not one of these fundamental rights. * * *

* * * *

The fact is that in deciding as it did—that "appointment of counsel is not a fundamental right, essential to a fair trial"—the Court in *Betts v. Brady* made an abrupt break with its own well-considered precedents. In returning to these old precedents, sounder we believe than the new, we but restore constitutional principles established to achieve a fair system of justice. Not only these precedents, but also reason and reflection require us to recognize that in our adversary system of criminal justice, any person haled into court, who is too poor to hire a lawyer, cannot be assured a fair trial unless counsel is provided for him. This seems to us to be an obvious truth. Governments, both state and federal, quite properly spend vast sums of money to establish machinery to try defendants accused of crime. Lawyers to prosecute are everywhere deemed essential to protect the public's interest in an orderly society. Similarly, there are few defendants charged with crime, few indeed, who fail to hire the best lawyers they can get to prepare and present their defenses. That government hires lawyers to prosecute and defendants who have the money hire lawyers to defend are the strongest indications of the widespread belief that lawyers in criminal courts are necessities, not luxuries. The right of one charged with crime to counsel may not be deemed fundamental and essential to fair trials in some countries, but it is in ours. From the very beginning, our state and national constitutions and laws have laid great emphasis on procedural and substantive safeguards designed to assure fair trials before impartial tribunals in which every defendant stands equal before the law. This noble ideal cannot be realized if the poor man charged with crime has to face his accusers without a lawyer to assist him. * * *

The Court in *Betts v. Brady* departed from the sound wisdom upon which the Court's holding in *Powell v. Alabama* rested. Florida, supported by two other States, has asked that *Betts v. Brady* be left intact. Twenty-two States, as friends of the Court, argue that *Betts* was "an anachronism when handed down" and that it should now be overruled. We agree.

Decision

The judgment is reversed and the cause is remanded to the Supreme Court of Florida for further action not inconsistent with this opinion.

GITLOW
v.
People of the State of **NEW YORK**
268 U.S. 652, 45 S.Ct. 625, 69 L.Ed. 1138.
Reargued Nov. 23, 1923.
Decided June 8, 1925.

Introduction

A free speech/bad-tendency rule case which allows First Amendment freedoms to be curtailed if there is a possibility that such expression might lead to some evil. In this case, a member of a left-wing group was convicted of violating New York State's criminal anarchy statute when he published and distributed materials urging the violent overthrow of the United States government.

WESTLAW Summary

Benjamin Gitlow was convicted of statutory crime of criminal anarchy. To review a judgment of the Court of Appeals of New York, affirming a judgment of the Appellate Division, he brings error. Judgment affirmed.

Case Excerpts

Mr. Justice SANFORD delivered the opinion of the Court.

Benjamin Gitlow was indicted in the Supreme Court of New York, with three others, for the statutory crime of criminal anarchy. He was separately tried, convicted, and sentenced to imprisonment. The judgment was affirmed by the Appellate Division and by the Court of

Appeals. The case is here on writ of error to the Supreme Court, to which the record was remitted.

The contention here is that the statute, by its terms and as applied in this case, is repugnant to the due process clause of the Fourteenth Amendment. * * *

* * * *

The following facts were established on the trial by undisputed evidence and admissions: The defendant is a member of the Left Wing Section of the Socialist Party, a dissenting branch or faction of that party formed in opposition to its dominant policy of "moderate Socialism." Membership in both is open to aliens as well as citizens. The Left Wing Section was organized nationally at a conference in New York City in June, 1919, attended by ninety delegates from twenty different States. The conference elected a National Council, of which the defendant was a member, and left to it the adoption of a "Manifesto." This was published in The Revolutionary Age, the official organ of the Left Wing. The defendant was on the board of managers of the paper and was its business manager. He arranged for the printing of the paper and took to the printer the manuscript of the first issue which contained the Left Wing Manifesto, and also a Communist Program and a Program of the Left Wing that had been adopted by the conference. Sixteen thousand copies were printed, which were delivered at the premises in New York City used as the office of the Revolutionary Age and the headquarters of the Left Wing, and occupied by the defendant and other officials. These copies were paid for by the defendant, as business manager of the paper. Employees at this office wrapped and mailed out copies of the paper under the defendant's direction; and copies were sold from this office. It was admitted that the defendant signed a card subscribing to the Manifesto and Program of the Left Wing, which all applicants were required to sign before being admitted to membership; that he went to different parts of the State to speak to branches of the Socialist Party about the principles of the Left Wing and advocated their adoption; and that he was responsible for the Manifesto as it appeared, that "he knew of the publication, in a general way and he knew of its publication afterwards, and is responsible for the circulation."

There was no evidence of any effect resulting from the publication and circulation of the Manifesto.

No witnesses were offered in behalf of the defendant.

* * * *

The Court of Appeals held that the Manifesto "advocated the overthrow of this government by violence, or by unlawful means." In one of the opinions representing the views of a majority of the court, it was said:

"It will be seen * * * that this defendant through the Manifesto * * * advocated the destruction of the state and the establishment of the dictatorship of the proletariat. * * * To advocate * * * the commission of this conspiracy or action by mass strike whereby government is crippled, the administration of justice paralyzed, and the health, morals and welfare of a community endangered, and this for the purpose of bringing about a revolution in the state, is to advocate the overthrow of organized government by unlawful means."

* * * *

The precise question presented, and the only question which we can consider under this writ of error, then is, whether the statute, as construed and applied in this case, by the State courts, deprived the defendant of his liberty of expression in violation of the due process clause of the Fourteenth Amendment.

The statute does not penalize the utterance or publication of abstract "doctrine" or academic discussion having no quality of incitement to any concrete action. It is not aimed against mere historical or philosophical essays. It does not restrain the advocacy of changes in the form of government by constitutional and lawful means. What it prohibits is language advocating, advising or teaching the overthrow of organized government by unlawful means. These words imply urging to action.

* * * *

For present purposes we may and do assume that freedom of speech and of the press—which are protected by the First Amendment from abridgment by Congress—are among the fundamental personal rights and "liberties" protected by the due process clause of the Fourteenth Amendment from impairment by the States. * * *

(1) It is a fundamental principle, long established, that the freedom of speech and of the press which is secured by the Constitution, does not confer an absolute right to speak or publish, without responsibility, whatever one may choose, or an unrestricted and unbridled license that gives immunity for every possible use of language and prevents the punishment of those who abuse this freedom. * * *

2) That a State in the exercise of its police power may punish those who abuse this freedom by utterances inimical to the public welfare, tending to corrupt public morals, incite to crime, or disturb the public peace, is not open to question. * * *

(3) And, for yet more imperative reasons, a State may punish utterances endangering the foundations of organized government and threatening its overthrow by unlawful means. These imperil its own existence as a constitutional State. * * *

(4, 5) By enacting the present statute the State has determined, through its legislative body, that utterances advocating the overthrow of organized government by force, violence and unlawful means, are so inimical to the general welfare and involve such danger of substantive evil that they may be penalized in the exercise of its police power. That determination must be given great weight. Every presumption is to be indulged in favor of the validity of the statute.

* * * *

6) We cannot hold that the present statute is an arbitrary or unreasonable exercise of the police power of the State unwarrantably infringing the freedom of speech or press; and we must and do sustain its constitutionality.

* * * *

The defendant's brief does not separately discuss any of the rulings of the trial court. It is only necessary to say that, applying the general rules already stated, we find that none of them involved any invasion of the constitutional rights of the defendant. It was not necessary, within the meaning of the statute, that the defendant should have advocated "some definite or immediate act or acts" of force, violence or unlawfulness. It was sufficient if such acts were advocated in general terms; and it was not essential that their immediate execution should have been advocated. Nor was it necessary that the language should have been "reasonably and ordinarily calculated to incite certain persons" to acts of force, violence or unlawfulness. The advocacy need not be addressed to specific persons. Thus, the publication and circulation of a newspaper article may be an encouragement or endeavor to persuade to murder, although not addressed to any person in particular.

We need not enter upon a consideration of the English common law rule of seditious libel or the Federal Sedition Act of 1798,11 to which reference is made in the defendant's brief. These are so unlike the present statute, that we think the decisions under them cast no helpful light upon the questions here.

Decision

And finding, for the reasons stated, that the statute is not in itself unconstitutional, and that it has not been applied in the present case in derogation of any constitutional right, the judgment of the Court of Appeals is Affirmed.

Barbara **GRUTTER**
v.
Lee **BOLLINGER** *et al.*
539 U.S. 306, 123 S.Ct. 2325, 156 L.Ed.2d 304
Argued April 1, 2003
Decided June 23, 2003

Introduction

In 1996, the University of Michigan Law School denied admission to Barbara Guttinger, a white Michigan resident with impressive academic qualifications. A year later, Guttinger filed suit, claiming that she had been unconstitutionally discriminated against because of her race. At the basis of her lawsuit was the law school's admission policy, which appeared to use race as a "predominant factor," giving preference to historically disadvantaged minorities such as African American and Hispanics at the expense of other racial groups such as whites and Asian Americans. To decide this case, the Court needed to determine whether the law school treated Guttinger and other similar applicants unequally because of their race.

WESTLAW Summary

Law school applicants who were denied admission challenged race-conscious admissions policy of state university law school, alleging that the admissions policy encouraging student body diversity violated their equal protection rights. The United States District Court for the Eastern District of Michigan, Bernard A. Friedman, J., held that the law school's consideration of race and ethnicity in its admissions decisions was unlawful and enjoined law school from using race as a factor in its admissions decisions. Appeal was taken. Sitting en banc, the United States Court of Appeals for the Sixth Circuit, Boyce F. Martin, Jr., Chief Judge, reversed the District Court's judgment and vacated the injunction. Certiorari was granted. The United States Supreme Court, Justice O'Connor, held that: (1) law school had a compelling interest in attaining a diverse student body; and (2) admissions program was narrowly tailored to serve its compelling interest in obtaining the educational benefits that flow from a diverse student body, and thus did not violate the Equal Protection Clause.

Case Excerpts

Justice O'CONNOR announced the judgment of the Court * * *.

This case requires us to decide whether the use of race as a factor in student admissions by the University of Michigan Law School (Law School) is unlawful.* * *

The hallmark of [the Law School's admission] policy is its focus on academic ability coupled with a flexible assessment of applicants' talents, experiences, and potential "to contribute to the learning of those around them." The policy requires admissions officials to evaluate each applicant based on all the information available in the file, including a personal statement, letters of recommendation, and an essay describing the ways in which the applicant will contribute to the life and diversity of the Law School. In reviewing an applicant's file, admissions officials must consider the applicant's undergraduate grade point average (GPA) and Law School Admissions Test (LSAT) score because they are important (if imperfect) predictors of academic success in law school. The policy stresses that "no applicant should be admitted unless we expect that applicant to do well enough to graduate with no serious academic problems."

The policy makes clear, however, that even the highest possible score does not guarantee admission to the Law School. Nor does a low score automatically disqualify an applicant.* * *

The policy aspires to "achieve that diversity which has the potential to enrich everyone's education and thus make a law school class stronger than the sum of its parts." The policy does not restrict the types of diversity contributions eligible for "substantial weight" in the admissions process, but instead recognizes "many possible bases for diversity admissions." The policy does, however, reaffirm the Law School's longstanding commitment to "one particular type of diversity," that is, "racial and ethnic diversity with special reference to the inclusion of students from groups which have been historically discriminated against, like African-Americans, Hispanics and Native Americans, who without this commitment might not be represented in our student body in meaningful numbers." By enrolling a " 'critical mass' of [underrepresented] minority students," the Law School seeks to "ensur[e] their ability to make unique contributions to the character of the Law School."

* * * *

Petitioner Barbara Grutter is a white Michigan resident who applied to the Law School in 1996 with a 3.8 grade point average and 161 LSAT score. The Law School initially placed petitioner on a waiting list, but subsequently rejected her application. In December 1997, petitioner filed suit . . . [alleging] that respondents discriminated against her on the basis of race in violation of the Fourteenth Amendment [and] Title VI of the Civil Rights Act of 1964.

Petitioner further alleged that her application was rejected because the Law School uses race as a "predominant" factor, giving applicants who belong to certain minority groups "a significantly greater chance of admission than students with similar credentials from disfavored racial groups." Petitioner also alleged that respondents "had no compelling interest to justify their use of race in the admissions process."

* * * *

During the 15-day bench trial [in District Court], the parties introduced extensive evidence concerning the Law School's use of race in the admissions process. Dennis Shields, Director of Admissions when petitioner applied to the Law School, testified that he did not direct his staff to admit a particular percentage or number of minority students, but rather to consider an applicant's race along with all other factors. Shields testified that at the height of the admissions season, he would frequently consult the so-called "daily reports" that kept track of the racial and ethnic composition of the class (along with other information such as residency status and gender). This was done, Shields testified, to ensure that a critical mass of underrepresented minority students would be reached so as to realize the educational benefits of a diverse student body.

Shields stressed, however, that he did not seek to admit any particular number or percentage of underrepresented minority students. * * * *.

We last addressed the use of race in public higher education over 25 years ago. In the landmark *Regents of the University of California v. Bakke* case, we reviewed a racial set-aside program that reserved 16 out of 100 seats in a medical school class for members of certain minority groups. * * * The only holding for the Court in *Bakke* was that a "State has a substantial interest that legitimately may be served by a properly devised admissions program involving the competitive consideration of race and ethnic origin."* * *

Since this Court's splintered decision in *Bakke,* Justice Powell's opinion announcing the judgment of the Court has served as the touchstone for constitutional analysis of race-conscious admissions policies. Public and private universities across the Nation have modeled their own admissions programs on Justice Powell's views on permissible race-conscious policies. . . . Justice Powell began by stating that "[t]he guarantee of equal protection cannot mean one thing when applied to one individual and something else when applied to a person of another color. If both are not accorded the same protection, then it is not equal." In Justice Powell's view, when governmental decisions "touch upon an individual's race or ethnic background, he is entitled to a judicial determination that the burden he is asked to bear on that basis is precisely tailored to serve a compelling governmental interest."* * *

Justice Powell approved the university's use of race to further only one interest: "the attainment of a diverse student body." With the important proviso that "constitutional limitations protecting individual rights may not be disregarded," Justice Powell grounded his analysis in the academic freedom that "long has been viewed as a special concern of the First Amendment." Justice Powell emphasized that nothing less than the " 'nation's future depends upon leaders trained through wide exposure' to the ideas and mores of students as diverse as this Nation of many peoples." * * *

Justice Powell was, however, careful to emphasize that in his view race "is only one element in a range of factors a university properly may consider in attaining the goal of a heterogeneous student body." For

Justice Powell, "[i]t is not an interest in simple ethnic diversity, in which a specified percentage of the student body is in effect guaranteed to be members of selected ethnic groups," that can justify the use of race. Rather, "[t]he diversity that furthers a compelling state interest encompasses a far broader array of qualifications and characteristics of which racial or ethnic origin is but a single though important element."
* * * *

The Equal Protection Clause provides that no State shall "deny to any person within its jurisdiction the equal protection of the laws." Because the Fourteenth Amendment "protect[s] *persons,* not *groups,*" all "governmental action based on race--a *group* classification long recognized as in most circumstances irrelevant and therefore prohibited--should be subjected to detailed judicial inquiry to ensure that the *personal* right to equal protection of the laws has not been infringed." * * *

We have held that all racial classifications imposed by government "must be analyzed by a reviewing court under strict scrutiny." This means that such classifications are constitutional only if they are narrowly tailored to further compelling governmental interests. * * * Although all governmental uses of race are subject to strict scrutiny, not all are invalidated by it. As we have explained, "whenever the government treats any person unequally because of his or her race, that person has suffered an injury that falls squarely within the language and spirit of the Constitution's guarantee of equal protection." But that observation "says nothing about the ultimate validity of any particular law; that determination is the job of the court applying strict scrutiny." When race-based action is necessary to further a compelling governmental interest, such action does not violate the constitutional guarantee of equal protection so long as the narrow-tailoring requirement is also satisfied.
* * * *

With these principles in mind, we turn to the question whether the Law School's use of race is justified by a compelling state interest. Before this Court, as they have throughout this litigation, respondents assert only one justification for their use of race in the admissions process: obtaining " the educational benefits that flow from a diverse student body." In other words, the Law School asks us to recognize, in the context of

higher education, a compelling state interest in student body diversity. * * * Today, we hold that the Law School has a compelling interest in attaining a diverse student body.
* * * *

Our conclusion that the Law School has a compelling interest in a diverse student body is informed by our view that attaining a diverse student body is at the heart of the Law School's proper institutional mission, and that "good faith" on the part of a university is "presumed" absent "a showing to the contrary."

As part of its goal of "assembling a class that is both exceptionally academically qualified and broadly diverse," the Law School seeks to "enroll a 'critical mass' of minority students." The Law School's interest is not simply "to assure within its student body some specified percentage of a particular group merely because of its race or ethnic origin." That would amount to outright racial balancing, which is patently unconstitutional. Rather, the Law School's concept of critical mass is defined by reference to the educational benefits that diversity is designed to produce.
* * * *

Here, the Law School engages in a highly individualized, holistic review of each applicant's file, giving serious consideration to all the ways an applicant might contribute to a diverse educational environment. The Law School affords this individualized consideration to applicants of all races. There is no policy, either *de jure* or *de facto,* of automatic acceptance or rejection based on any single "soft" variable. . . . . [T]he Law School's admissions policy "is flexible enough to consider all pertinent elements of diversity in light of the particular qualifications of each applicant, and to place them on the same footing for consideration, although not necessarily according them the same weight."

Decision

The judgment of the Court of Appeals for the Sixth Circuit, accordingly, is affirmed.
It is so ordered.

Richard Perry **LOVING**
v.
COMMONWEALTH OF VIRGINIA
388 U. S. 1, 87 S.Ct. 1817, 18 L.Ed.2d 1010.
Argued April 10, 1967.
Decided June 12, 1967.

Introduction

A civil rights case in which a state statute banning interracial marriages was declared unconstitutional.

WESTLAW Summary

Proceeding on motion to vacate sentences for violating state ban on interracial marriages. The Circuit Court of Caroline County, Virginia, denied motion, and writ of error was granted. The Virginia Supreme Court of Appeals affirmed the convictions, and probable jurisdiction was noted. The United States Supreme Court, Mr. Chief Justice Warren, held that miscegenation statutes adopted by Virginia to prevent marriages between persons solely on basis of racial classification violate equal protection and due process clauses of Fourteenth Amendment.

Case Excerpts

Mr. Chief Justice WARREN delivered the opinion of the Court.

This case presents a constitutional question never addressed by this Court: whether a statutory scheme adopted by the State of Virginia to prevent marriages between persons solely on the basis of racial classifications violates the Equal Protection and Due Process Clauses of the Fourteenth Amendment. For reasons which seem to us to reflect the central meaning of those constitutional commands, we conclude that these statutes cannot stand consistently with the Fourteenth Amendment.

In June 1958, two residents of Virginia, Mildred Jeter, a Negro woman, and Richard Loving, a white man, were married in the District of Columbia pursuant to its laws. Shortly after their marriage, the Lovings returned to Virginia and established their marital abode in Caroline County. At the October Term, 1958, of the Circuit Court of Caroline County, a grand jury issued an indictment charging the Lovings with violating Virginia's ban on interracial marriages. On January 6, 1959, the Lovings pleaded guilty to the charge and were sentenced to one year in jail; however, the trial judge suspended the sentence for a period of 25 years on the condition that the Lovings leave the State and not return to Virginia together for 25 years. * * *

After their convictions, the Lovings took up residence in the District of Columbia. * * * [On] October 28, 1964, the Lovings instituted a class action in the United States District Court for the Eastern District of Virginia requesting that a three-judge court be convened to declare the Virginia antimiscegenation statutes unconstitutional and to enjoin state officials from enforcing their convictions. On January 22, 1965, the state trial judge denied the motion to vacate the sentences, and the Lovings perfected an appeal to the Supreme Court of Appeals of Virginia. * * *

The Supreme Court of Appeals upheld the constitutionality of the antimiscegenation statutes and, after modifying the sentence, affirmed the convictions. The Lovings appealed this decision * * *

The two statutes under which appellants were convicted and sentenced are part of a comprehensive statutory scheme aimed at prohibiting and punishing interracial marriages. * * *

Virginia is now one of 16 States which prohibit and punish marriages on the basis of racial classifications. Penalties for miscegenation arose as an incident to slavery and have been common in Virginia since the colonial period. * * *

In upholding the constitutionality of these provisions in the decision below, the Supreme Court of Appeals of Virginia * * * reasoned that marriage has traditionally been subject to state regulation without federal intervention, and, consequently, the regulation of marriage should be left to exclusive state control by the Tenth Amendment.

While the state court is no doubt correct in asserting that marriage is a social relation subject to the State's police power, * * * the State does not contend in its argument before this Court that its powers to regulate marriage are unlimited notwithstanding the commands of the Fourteenth Amendment. * * * [T]he State contends that, because its miscegenation statutes punish equally both the white and the Negro participants in an interracial marriage, these statutes, despite their reliance on racial classifications do not constitute an invidious discrimination based upon race. The second argument advanced by the State assumes the validity of its equal application theory. The argument is that, if the Equal Protection Clause does not outlaw miscegenation statutes because of their reliance on racial classifications, the question of constitutionality would thus become whether there was any rational basis for a State to treat interracial marriages differently from other marriages. On this question, the State argues, the scientific evidence is substantially in doubt and, consequently, this Court should defer to the wisdom of the state legislature in adopting its policy of discouraging interracial marriages.

Because we reject the notion that the mere "equal application" of a statute containing racial classifications is enough to remove the classifications from the Fourteenth Amendment's proscription of all invidious racial discriminations, we do not accept the State's contention that these statutes should be upheld if there is any possible basis for concluding that they serve a rational purpose. * * * [T]he fact of equal application does not immunize the statute from the very heavy burden of justification which the Fourteenth Amendment has traditionally required of state statutes drawn according to race.

* * * *

* * * Over the years, this Court has consistently repudiated "(d)istinctions between citizens solely because of their ancestry" as being "odious to a free people whose institutions are founded upon the doctrine of equality." At the very least, the Equal Protection Clause demands that racial classifications, especially suspect in criminal

statutes, be subjected to the "most rigid scrutiny," and, if they are ever to be upheld, they must be shown to be necessary to the accomplishment of some permissible state objective, independent of the racial discrimination which it was the object of the Fourteenth Amendment to eliminate. * * *

There is patently no legitimate overriding purpose independent of invidious racial discrimination, which justifies this classification. The fact that Virginia prohibits only interracial marriages involving white persons demonstrates that the racial classifications must stand on their own justification, as measures designed to maintain White Supremacy. We have consistently denied the constitutionality of measures which restrict the rights of citizens on account of race. There can be no doubt that restricting the freedom to marry solely because of racial classifications violates the central meaning of the Equal Protection Clause.

These statutes also deprive the Lovings of liberty without due process of law in violation of the Due Process Clause of the Fourteenth Amendment. * * *

Marriage is one of the "basic civil rights of man," fundamental to our very existence and survival. To deny this fundamental freedom on so unsupportable a basis as the racial classifications embodied in these statutes, classifications so directly subversive of the principle of equality at the heart of the Fourteenth Amendment, is surely to deprive all the State's citizens of liberty without due process of law. The Fourteenth Amendment requires that the freedom of choice to marry not be restricted by invidious racial discriminations. Under our Constitution, the freedom to marry or not marry, a person of another race resides with the individual and cannot be infringed by the State.

Decision

These convictions must be reversed. It is so ordered.

Dollree **MAPP**
v.
OHIO
367 U.S. 643, 81 S.Ct. 1684, 6 L.Ed.2d 1081.
Supreme Court of the United States.
Argued March 29, 1961.
Decided June 19, 1961.

Introduction

Under the exclusionary rule, any evidence obtained in violation of an accused's constitutional rights, under the Fourth, Fifth, and Sixth Amendments, is not admissible in court. At one time, this rule applied only to the federal government. In this case, the Supreme Court held that the exclusionary rule could be applied in state criminal trials to bar the admissibility of evidence that is the product of improper searches and seizures.

WESTLAW Summary

Prosecution for possession and control of obscene material. An Ohio Common Pleas Court rendered judgment, and the defendant appealed. The Ohio Supreme Court affirmed the judgment, and the defendant again appealed. The Supreme Court, Mr. Justice Clark, held that evidence obtained by unconstitutional search was inadmissible and vitiated conviction.

Case Excerpts

Mr. Justice CLARK delivered the opinion of the Court.

* * * *
* * * Today we * * * close the only courtroom door remaining open to evidence secured by official lawlessness in flagrant abuse of [the right under the Fourth Amendment to be free from unreasonable

searches and seizures], reserved to all persons as a specific guarantee against that very same unlawful conduct. We hold that all evidence obtained by searches and seizures in violation of the Constitution is, by that same authority, inadmissible in a state court.

* * * *

Since the Fourth Amendment's right of privacy has been declared enforceable against the States through the Due Process Clause [a provision of the Fourteenth Amendment that guarantees no person shall be deprived of life, liberty, or property without due process] * * *, it is enforceable against them by the same sanction of exclusion as is used against the Federal Government. Were it otherwise, then * * * the freedom from state invasions of privacy would be so ephemeral [short] and so neatly severed from its conceptual nexus [connection] with the freedom from all brutish means of coercing evidence as not to merit this Court's high regard as a freedom implicit in the concept of ordered liberty. * * * To hold otherwise is to grant the right but in reality to withhold its privilege and enjoyment. * * *

Indeed, we are aware of no restraint, similar to that rejected today, conditioning the enforcement of any other basic constitutional right. The right to privacy, no less important than any other right carefully and particularly reserved to the people, would stand in marked contrast to all other rights declared as basic to a free society. This Court has not hesitated to enforce as strictly against the States as it does against the Federal Government the rights of free speech and of a free press, the rights to notice and to a fair, public trial, including, as it does, the right not to be convicted by use of a coerced confession, however logically relevant it be, and without regard to its reliability. And nothing could be more certain than that when a coerced confession is involved, the relevant rules of evidence are overridden without regard to the incidence of such conduct by the police, slight or frequent. Why should not the same rule apply to what is tantamount [equal in effect or value] to coerced testimony by way of unconstitutional seizure of goods, papers, effects, documents, etc.? * * *

* * * *

Moreover, our holding that the exclusionary rule is an essential part of both the Fourth and Fourteenth Amendments is not only the logical dictate of prior cases, but it also makes very good sense. There is no war between the Constitution and common sense. Presently, a federal prosecutor may make no use of evidence illegally seized, but a State's attorney across the street may, although he supposedly is operating under the enforceable prohibitions of the same Amendment. Thus the State, by admitting evidence unlawfully seized, serves to encourage disobedience to the Federal Constitution which it is bound to uphold. * * * In nonexclusionary States, federal officers, being human, were by it invited to and did, as our cases indicate, step across the street to the State's attorney with their unconstitutionally seized evidence. Prosecution on the basis of that evidence was then had in a state court in utter disregard of the enforceable Fourth Amendment. If the fruits of an unconstitutional search had been inadmissible in both state and federal courts, this inducement to evasion would have been sooner eliminated. * * *

Federal-state cooperation in the solution of crime under constitutional standards will be promoted, if only by recognition of their now mutual obligation to respect the same fundamental criteria in their approaches. However much in a particular case insistence upon such rules may appear as a technicality that inures to the benefit of a guilty person, the history of the criminal law proves that tolerance of shortcut methods in law enforcement impairs its enduring effectiveness. * * *

There are those who say, as did Justice (then Judge) Cardozo, that under our constitutional exclusionary doctrine "[t]he criminal is to go free because the constable has blundered." In some cases this will undoubtedly be the result. But there is another consideration—the imperative of judicial integrity. The criminal goes free, if he must, but it is the law that sets him free. Nothing can destroy a government more quickly than its failure to observe its own laws, or worse, its disregard of the charter of its own existence. * * *

The ignoble shortcut to conviction left open to the State tends to destroy the entire system of constitutional restraints on which the liberties of the people rest. Having once recognized that the right to privacy embodied in the Fourth Amendment is enforceable against the States, and that the right to be secure against rude invasions of privacy by state officers is, therefore, constitutional in origin, we can no longer permit that right to remain an empty promise. Because it is enforceable in the same manner and to like effect as other basic rights secured by the Due Process Clause, we can no longer permit it to be revocable at the whim of any police officer who, in the name of law enforcement itself, chooses to suspend its enjoyment. Our decision, founded on reason and truth, gives to the individual no more than that which the Constitution guarantees him, to the police officer no less than that to which honest law enforcement is entitled, and, to the courts, that judicial integrity so necessary in the true administration of justice.

The judgment of the Supreme Court of Ohio is reversed and the cause remanded [sent back] for further proceedings not inconsistent with this opinion.

Decision

The Court reversed the decision of the Ohio Supreme Court and remanded the case for further proceedings consistent with this opinion.

William **MARBURY**
v.
James **MADISON**, Secretary of State of the United States
5 U.S. 137, 1 Cranch 137, 2 L.Ed. 60.
Supreme Court of the United States.
Decided February Term, 1803.

Introduction

This decision stands for the principle of judicial review (the power of the courts to decide whether a law is constitutional). The Supreme Court had to decide whether to order James Madison, the secretary of state, to deliver the previous administration's letters of commission to judicial appointees. The Court's dilemma: If it ordered the commissions delivered, Madison could refuse, and the Court had no way to compel delivery. If the Court allowed the new administration to do as it wished, however, the Court's power would be severely eroded.

Text Authors' Summary

John Adams lost his bid for reelection to Thomas Jefferson in 1800. At the end of his term, Adams tried to "pack" the judiciary with Federalists (members of Adams's political party). Of fifty-nine appointment letters, only forty-two were delivered before Jefferson took office. William Marbury and others who had not received their appointments asked the United States Supreme Court to order the delivery of the letters. The Supreme Court ruled that under the Constitution, it did not have the authority to order the delivery, because the statute authorizing it to issue such an order was unconstitutional.

Case Excerpts

Mr. Chief Justice MARSHALL delivered the opinion of the Court.

* * * *

* * * That the people have an original right to establish, for their future government, such principles as, in their opinion, shall most conduce to their own happiness, is the basis on which the whole American fabric has been erected. The exercise of this original right is a very great exertion; nor can it nor ought it to be frequently repeated. The principles, therefore, so established [in the Constitution] are deemed fundamental. And as the authority, from which they proceed, is supreme, and can seldom act, they are designed to be permanent.

This original and supreme will organizes the government, and assigns to different departments their respective powers. It may either stop here; or establish certain limits not to be transcended by those departments. The government of the United States is of the latter description. The powers of the legislature are defined and limited; and that those limits may not be mistaken or forgotten, the constitution is written. To what purpose are powers limited, and to what purpose is that limitation committed to writing; if these limits may, at any time, be passed by those intended to be restrained? The distinction between a government with limited and unlimited powers is abolished, if those limits do not confine the persons on whom they are imposed, and if acts prohibited and acts allowed are of equal obligation. It is a proposition too plain to be contested, that the constitution controls any legislative act repugnant to it; or, that the legislature may alter the constitution by an ordinary act.

Between these alternatives there is no middle ground. The constitution is either a superior, paramount law, unchangeable by ordinary means, or it is on a level with ordinary legislative acts, and like other acts, is alterable when the legislature shall please to alter it. If the former part of the alternative be true, then a legislative act contrary to the constitution is not law: if the latter part be true, then written constitutions are absurd attempts, on the part of the people, to limit a power in its own nature illimitable.

Certainly all those who have framed written constitutions contemplate them as forming the fundamental and paramount law of the nation, and consequently the theory of every such government must be, that an act of the legislature repugnant to the constitution is void. This theory is essentially attached to a written constitution, and is consequently to be considered by this court as one of the fundamental principles of our society. It is not therefore to be lost sight of in the further consideration of this subject.

If an act of the legislature, repugnant to the constitution, is void, does it, notwithstanding its invalidity, bind the courts and oblige them to give it effect? Or, in other words, though it be not law, does it constitute a rule as operative as if it was a law? This would be to overthrow in fact what was established in theory; and would seem, at first view, an absurdity too gross to be insisted on. It shall, however, receive a more attentive consideration.

It is emphatically the province and duty of the judicial department to say what the law is. Those who apply the rule to particular cases, must of necessity expound and interpret that rule. If two laws conflict with each other, the courts must decide on the operation of each. So if a law be in opposition to the constitution: if both the law and the constitution apply to a particular case, so that the court must either decide that case conformably to the law, disregarding the constitution; or conformably to the constitution, disregarding the law: the court must determine which of these conflicting rules governs the case. This is of the very essence of judicial duty. If then the courts are to regard the constitution; and he constitution is superior to any ordinary act of the legislature; the constitution, and not such ordinary act, must govern the case to which they both apply.

Those then who controvert the principle that the constitution is to be considered, in court, as a paramount law, are reduced to the necessity of maintaining that courts must close their eyes on the constitution, and see only the law. This doctrine would subvert the very foundation of all written constitutions. It would declare that an act, which, according to the principles and theory of our government, is entirely void, is yet, in practice, completely obligatory. It would declare, that if the legislature shall do what is expressly forbidden, such act, notwithstanding the express prohibition, is in reality effectual. It would be giving to the legislature a practical and real omnipotence with the same breath which professes to restrict their powers within narrow limits. It is prescribing limits, and declaring that those limits may be passed at pleasure. That it thus reduces to nothing what we have deemed the greatest improvement on political institutions—a written constitution, would of itself be sufficient, in America where written constitutions have been viewed with so much reverence, for rejecting the construction. But the peculiar expressions of the constitution of the United States furnish additional arguments in favor of its rejection. The judicial power of the United States is extended to all cases arising under the constitution. Could it be the intention of those who gave this power, to say that, in using it, the constitution should not be looked into? That a case arising under the constitution should be decided without examining the instrument under which it arises? This is too extravagant to be maintained. In some cases then, the constitution must be looked into by the judges. And if they can open it at all, what part of it are they forbidden to read, or to obey?

* * * *

* * * [I]t is apparent, that the framers of the constitution contemplated that instrument as a rule for the government of courts, as well as of the legislature. Why otherwise does it direct the judges to take an oath to support it? This oath certainly applies, in an especial manner, to their conduct in their official character. How immoral to impose it on them, if they were to be used as the instruments, and the knowing instruments, for violating what they swear to support!

* * * *

If such be the real state of things, this is worse than solemn mockery. To prescribe, or to take this oath, becomes equally a crime.

It is also not entirely unworthy of observation, that in declaring what shall be the supreme law of the land, the constitution itself is first mentioned; and not the laws of the United States generally, but those only which shall be made in pursuance of the constitution, have that rank.

Thus, the particular phraseology of the constitution of the United States confirms and strengthens the principle, supposed to be essential to all written constitutions, that a law repugnant to the constitution is void, and that courts, as well as other departments, are bound by that instrument.

The rule must be discharged.

Decision

The Court refused to order the delivery of the letters.

McCULLOCH
v.
State of **MARYLAND**
17 U.S. 316, 4 Wheat. 316, 4 L.Ed. 579.
Supreme Court of the United States.
Decided February Term, 1819.

Introduction

The question in this case was whether Congress had the power to incorporate a bank. This question concerned the distribution of power between the federal government and the states: Did Congress have only those powers listed in the Constitution, or could Congress do whatever might be logically implied from those powers? The Supreme Court held that the Constitution did not limit the power of the national government but allowed for its expansion.

Text Authors' Summary

Congress chartered the Bank of the United States. The state of Maryland enacted a law imposing a tax on the bank. James McCulloch, the cashier of the Baltimore branch of the bank, was convicted in a Maryland state court and fined for not paying the tax. This Maryland Court of Appeals upheld this conviction. McCulloch appealed his conviction to the United States Supreme Court. The Supreme Court refused to invalidate the act of Congress that incorporated the Bank of the United States.

Case Excerpts

MARSHALL, Ch. J. [Chief Justice], delivered the opinion of the Court.

* * * *
* * * [T]he counsel for the state of Maryland have deemed it of some importance, in the construction of the constitution, to consider that

instrument, not as emanating from the people, but as the act of sovereign and independent states. * * * The convention which framed the constitution was indeed elected by the state legislatures. But the instrument, when it came from their hands, was a mere proposal, without obligation, or pretensions to it. It was reported to the then existing congress of the United States, with a request that it might "be submitted to a convention of delegates, chosen in each state by the people thereof, under the recommendation of its legislature, for their assent and ratification." This mode of proceeding was adopted; and by the convention, by congress, and by the state legislatures, the instrument was submitted to the people. * * *

From these conventions, the constitution derives its whole authority. * * * [T]he people were at perfect liberty to accept or reject it; and their act was final. It required not the affirmance, and could not be negatived, by the state governments. * * *

* * * The government of the Union, then * * *, is, emphatically and truly, a government of the people. In form, and in substance, it emanates from them. Its powers are granted by them, and are to be exercised directly on them, and for their benefit.

This government is acknowledged by all, to be one of enumerated powers. * * * But the question respecting the extent of the powers actually granted, is perpetually arising, and will probably continue to arise, so long as our system shall exist.

In discussing these questions, the conflicting powers of the general and state governments must be brought into view, and the supremacy of their respective laws, when they are in opposition, must be settled.
* * * *

The government of the United States, * * * though limited in its powers, is supreme; and its laws, when made in pursuance of the constitution, form the supreme law of the land * * *.

Among the enumerated powers, we do not find that of establishing a bank or creating a corporation. But there is no phrase in the instrument which * * * excludes incidental or implied powers; and which requires that everything granted shall be expressly and minutely described. * * * A constitution, to contain an accurate detail of all the subdivisions of which its great powers will admit, and of all the means by which they may be carried into execution, would partake of the prolixity [length] of a legal code, and could scarcely be embraced by the human mind. It would, probably, never be understood by the public. Its nature, therefore, requires, that only its great outlines should be marked, its important objects designated, and the minor ingredients which compose those objects, be deduced from the nature of the objects themselves. * * * [W]e must never forget that it is a constitution we are expounding.

* * * *

* * * [T]he constitution of the United States has not left the right of congress to employ the necessary means, for the execution of the powers conferred on the government, to general reasoning. To its enumeration of powers is added, that of making "all laws which shall be necessary and proper, for carrying into execution the foregoing powers, and all other powers vested by this constitution, in the government of the United States, or in any department thereof.".]

* * * *

* * * It must have been the intention of those who gave these powers, to insure, so far as human prudence could insure, their beneficial execution. This could not be done, by confiding the choice of means to such narrow limits as not to leave it in the power of congress to adopt any which might be appropriate, and which were conducive to the end. This provision is made in a constitution, intended to endure for ages to come, and consequently, to be adapted to the various crises of human affairs. To have prescribed the means by which government should, in all future time, execute its powers, would have been to change, entirely, the character of the instrument, and give it the properties of a legal code. It would have been an unwise attempt to provide, by immutable rules, for exigencies [urgent needs] which, if foreseen at all, must have been seen dimly, and which can be best provided for as they occur. To have declared, that the best means shall not be used, but those alone, without which the power given would be nugatory [unimportant], would have been to deprive the legislature of the capacity to avail itself of experience, to exercise its reason, and to accommodate its legislation to circumstances. * * *

* * * *

* * *[The necessary and proper clause was not intended to limit Congress's power to legislate] for the following reasons: 1st. The clause is placed among the powers of congress, not among the limitations on those powers. 2d. Its terms purport to enlarge, not to diminish the powers vested in the government. It purports to be an additional power, not a restriction on those already granted. * * * If * * * [the framers'] intention had been, by this clause, to restrain the free use of means which might otherwise have been implied, that intention would have been inserted in another place, and would have been expressed in [other] terms * * *. Had the intention been to make this clause restrictive, it would unquestionably have been so in form as well as in effect.

* * * *

We admit, as all must admit, that the powers of the government are limited, and that its limits are not to be transcended. But we think the sound construction of the constitution must allow to the national legislature that discretion, with respect to the means by which the powers it confers are to be carried into execution, which will enable that body to perform the high duties assigned to it, in the manner most beneficial to the people. Let the end be legitimate, let it be within the scope of the constitution, and all means which are appropriate, which are plainly adapted to that end, which are not prohibited, but consist with the letter and spirit of the constitution, are constitutional.

* * * *

After the most deliberate consideration, it is the unanimous and decided opinion of this court, that the act to incorporate the Bank of the United States is a law made in pursuance of the constitution, and is a part of the supreme law of the land.

Decision

The Court reversed the Maryland court's decision.

Marvin **MILLER**
v.
State of **CALIFORNIA**
413 U.S. 15, 93 S.Ct. 2607, 37 L.Ed.2d 419.
Argued Jan. 18-19, 1972.
Reargued Nov. 7, 1972.
Decided June 21, 1973.
Rehearing Denied Oct. 9, 1973.

Introduction

A freedom of speech/obscenity case in which the Court created a formal list of requirements as a test of obscenity that must be meet for material to be legally obscene. They are that (1) the average person finds that it violates contemporary community standards, (2) the work taken as a whole appeals to prurient interest in sex, (3) the work shows patently offensive sexual conduct, and (4) the work lacks serious redeeming literary, artistic, political, or scientific merit.

WESTLAW Summary

Defendant was convicted of mailing unsolicited sexually explicit material in violation of a California statute, and the Appellate Department, Superior Court of California, County of Orange, affirmed and defendant appealed. The Supreme Court held that a work may be subject to state regulation where that work, taken as a whole, appeals to the prurient interest in sex; portrays, in a patently offensive way, sexual conduct specifically defined by the applicable state law; and, taken as a whole, does not have serious literary, artistic, political or scientific value. The Court also rejected the test of "utterly without redeeming social value" as a constitutional standard.

Case Excerpts

Mr. Chief Justice BURGER delivered the opinion of the Court.
* * * *

Appellant conducted a mass mailing campaign to advertise the sale of illustrated books, euphemistically called "adult" material. After a jury trial, he was convicted of violating California Penal Code [Section] 311.2(a), a misdemeanor, by knowingly distributing obscene matter, and the Appellate Department, Superior Court of California, County of Orange, summarily affirmed the judgment without opinion. Appellant's conviction was specifically based on his conduct in causing five unsolicited advertising brochures to be sent through the mail in an envelope addressed to a restaurant in Newport Beach, California. The envelope was opened by the manager of the restaurant and his mother. They had not requested the brochures; they complained to the police.
* * * *

This case involves the application of a State's criminal obscenity statute to a situation in which sexually explicit materials have been thrust by aggressive sales action upon unwilling recipients who had in no way indicated any desire to receive such materials. This Court has recognized that the States have a legitimate interest in prohibiting dissemination or exhibition of obscene material when the mode of dissemination carries with it a significant danger of offending the sensibilities of unwilling recipients or of exposure to juveniles. It is in this context that we are called on to define the standards which must be used to identify obscene material that a State may regulate without infringing on the First Amendment as applicable to the States through the Fourteenth Amendment.
* * * *

" * * * There are certain well-defined and narrowly limited classes of speech, the prevention and punishment of which have never been thought to raise any Constitutional problem. These include the lewd and obscene . . . . It has been well observed that such utterances are no essential part of any exposition of ideas, and are of such slight social value as a step to truth that any benefit that may be derived from them is clearly outweighed by the social interest in order and morality . . . . "

This much has been categorically settled by the Court, that obscene material is unprotected by the First Amendment. We acknowledge, however, the inherent dangers of undertaking to regulate any form of expression. State statutes designed to regulate obscene materials must be carefully limited. As a result, we now confine the permissible scope of such regulation to works which depict or describe sexual conduct. That conduct must be specifically defined by the applicable state law, as written or authoritatively construed. A state offense must also be limited to works which, taken as a whole, appeal to the prurient interest in sex, which portray sexual conduct in a patently offensive way, and which, taken as a whole, do not have serious literary, artistic, political, or scientific value.

The basic guidelines for the trier of fact must be: (a) whether "the average person, applying contemporary community standards" would find that the work, taken as a whole, appeals to the prurient interest; (b) whether the work depicts or describes, in a patently offensive way, sexual conduct specifically defined by the applicable state law; and (c) whether the work, taken as a whole, lacks serious literary, artistic, political, or scientific value. * * *

Under the holdings announced today, no one will be subject to prosecution for the sale or exposure of obscene materials unless these materials depict or describe patently offensive "hard core" sexual conduct specifically defined by the regulating state law, as written or construed. We are satisfied that these specific prerequisites will provide fair notice to a dealer in such materials that his public and commercial activities may bring prosecution. If the inability to define regulated materials with ultimate, god-like precision altogether removes the power of the States or the Congress to regulate, then "hard core" pornography may be exposed without limit to the juvenile, the passerby, and the consenting adult alike * * *.

* * * *

Under a National Constitution, fundamental First Amendment limitations on the powers of the States do not vary from community to community, but this does not mean that there are, or should or can be, fixed, uniform national standards of precisely what appeals to the "prurient interest" or is "patently offensive." These are essentially questions of fact, and our Nation is simply too big and too diverse for this Court to reasonably expect that such standards could be articulated for all 50 States in a single formulation, even assuming the prerequisite consensus exists. When triers of fact are asked to decide whether "the average person, applying contemporary community standards" would consider certain materials "prurient," it would be unrealistic to require that the answer be based on some abstract formulation. The adversary system, with lay jurors as the usual ultimate factfinders in criminal prosecutions, has historically permitted triers of fact to draw on the standards of their community, guided always by limiting instructions on the law. To require a State to structure obscenity proceedings around evidence of a national "community standard" would be an exercise in futility.

* * * *

In sum, we (a) reaffirm * * * that obscene material is not protected by the First Amendment; (b) hold that such material can be regulated by the States, subject to the specific safeguards enunciated above, without a showing that the material is "utterly without redeeming social value"; and (c) hold that obscenity is to be determined by applying "contemporary community standards," not "national standards.'" The judgment of the Appellate Department of the Superior Court, Orange County, California, is vacated and the case remanded to that court for further proceedings not inconsistent with the First Amendment standards established by this opinion.

Decision

Vacated and remanded.

Ernesto A. **MIRANDA**
v.
State of **ARIZONA**
384 U.S. 436, 86 S.Ct. 1602, 16 L.Ed.2d 694.
Argued Feb. 28, 1966.
Decided June 13, 1966.

Introduction

A rights of the accused's right to remain silent case in which a mentally disturbed suspect, Ernesto Miranda, had been arrested, questioned for two hours, and confessed to the crime of kidnapping and rape. His conviction was reversed by the Supreme Court on the basis of the Fifth and Sixth Amendments. Now people are read their "Miranda rights," which include the right to remain silent.

WESTLAW Summary

Criminal prosecution. The Superior Court, Maricopa County, Arizona, rendered judgment, and the Supreme Court of Arizona affirmed. The defendant obtained certiorari. The Supreme Court held that statements obtained from defendants during incommunicado interrogation in police-dominated atmosphere, without full warning of constitutional rights, were inadmissible as having been obtained in violation of Fifth Amendment privilege against self-incrimination.

Case Excerpts

Mr. Chief Justice WARREN delivered the opinion of the Court.

[On March 13, 1963, petitioner, Ernesto Miranda, was arrested at his home and taken in custody to a Phoenix police station. He was there identified by the complaining witness. The police then took him to "Interrogation Room No. 2" of the detective bureau. There he was questioned by two police officers. The officers admitted at trial that Miranda was not advised that he had a right to have an attorney present. Two hours later, the officers emerged from the interrogation room with a written confession signed by Miranda. At the top of the statement was a typed paragraph stating that the confession was made voluntarily, without threats or promises of immunity and "with full knowledge of my legal rights, understanding any statement I make may be used against me.'"

At his trial before a jury, the written confession was admitted into evidence over the objection of defense counsel, and the officers testified to the prior oral confession made by Miranda during the interrogation. Miranda was found guilty of kidnapping and rape. He was sentenced to 20 to 30 years' imprisonment on each count, the sentences to run concurrently. On appeal, the Supreme Court of Arizona held that Miranda's constitutional rights were not violated in obtaining the confession and affirmed the conviction. In reaching its decision, the court emphasized heavily the fact that Miranda did not specifically request counsel.

The case before us raises questions which go to the roots of our concepts of American criminal jurisprudence: the restraints society must observe consistent with the Federal Constitution in prosecuting individuals for crime. More specifically, we deal with the admissibility of statements obtained from an individual who is subjected to custodial police interrogation and the necessity for procedures which assure that the individual is accorded his privilege under the Fifth Amendment to the Constitution not to be compelled to incriminate himself.

* * * *

* * * While the admissions or confessions of the prisoner, when voluntarily and freely made, have always ranked high in the scale of incriminating evidence, if an accused person be asked to explain his apparent connection with a crime under investigation, the ease with which the questions put to him may assume an inquisitorial character, the temptation to press the witness unduly, to browbeat him if he be timid or reluctant, to push him into a corner, and to entrap him into fatal contradictions, which is so painfully evident in many of the earlier state trials * * *.

* * * *

Our holding will be spelled out with some specificity in the pages which follow but briefly stated it is this: the prosecution may not use statements, whether exculpatory or inculpatory, stemming from custodial interrogation of the defendant unless it demonstrates the use of procedural safeguards effective to secure the privilege against self-incrimination. By custodial interrogation, we mean questioning initiated by law enforcement officers after a person has been taken into custody or otherwise deprived of his freedom of action in any significant way. As for the procedural safeguards to be employed, unless other fully effective means are devised to inform accused persons of their right of silence and to assure a continuous opportunity to exercise it, the following measures are required. Prior to any questioning, the person must be warned that he has a right to remain silent, that any statement he does make may be used as evidence against him, and that he has a right to the presence of an attorney, either retained or appointed. The defendant may waive effectuation of these rights, provided the waiver is made voluntarily, knowingly and intelligently. If, however, he indicates in any manner and at any stage of the process that he wishes to consult with an attorney before speaking there can be no questioning. Likewise, if the individual is alone and indicates in any manner that he does not wish to be interrogated, the police may not question him. The mere fact that he may have answered some questions or volunteered some statements on his own does not deprive him of the right to refrain from answering any further inquiries until he has consulted with an attorney and thereafter consents to be questioned.

* * * *

In [this case], we might not find the defendant's statements to have been involuntary in traditional terms. Our concern for adequate safeguards to protect precious Fifth Amendment rights is, of course, not lessened in the slightest. In each of the cases, the defendant was thrust into an unfamiliar atmosphere and run through menacing police interrogation procedures. The potentiality for compulsion is forcefully apparent [in this case] where the indigent Mexican defendant was a seriously disturbed individual with pronounced sexual fantasies * * *. To be sure, the records do not evince overt physical coercion or patent psychological ploys. The fact remains that * * * the officers [did not] undertake to afford appropriate safeguards at the outset of the interrogation to insure that the statements were truly the product of free choice.

It is obvious that such an interrogation environment is created for no purpose other than to subjugate the individual to the will of his examiner. This atmosphere carries its own badge of intimation. To be sure, this is not physical intimidation, but it is equally destructive of human dignity. The current practice of incommunicado interrogation is at odds with one of our Nation's most cherished principles—that the individual may not be compelled to incriminate himself. Unless adequate protective devices are employed to dispel the compulsion inherent in custodial surroundings, no statement obtained from the defendant can truly be the product of his free choice. * * *
* * * *

The question in [this case] is whether the privilege is fully applicable during a period of custodial interrogation. In this Court, the privilege has consistently been accorded a liberal construction. We are satisfied that all the principles embodied in the privilege apply to informal compulsion exerted by law-enforcement officers during in-custody questioning. An individual swept from familiar surroundings into police custody, surrounded by antagonistic forces, and subjected to the techniques of persuasion described above cannot be otherwise than under compulsion to speak. As a practical matter, the compulsion to speak in the isolated setting of the police station may well be greater than in courts or other official investigations, where there are often impartial observers to guard against intimidation or trickery.
* * * *

Today, then, there can be no doubt that the Fifth Amendment privilege is available outside of criminal court proceedings and serves to protect persons in all settings in which their freedom of action is curtailed in any significant way from being compelled to incriminate themselves. We have concluded that without proper safeguards the process of in-custody interrogation of persons suspected or accused of crime contains inherently compelling pressures which work to undermine the individual's will to resist and to compel him to speak where he would not otherwise do so freely. In order to combat these pressures and to permit a full opportunity to exercise the privilege against self-incrimination, the accused must be adequately and effectively apprised of his rights and the exercise of those rights must be fully honored.

* * * *

To summarize, we hold that when an individual is taken into custody or otherwise deprived of his freedom by the authorities in any significant way and is subjected to questioning, the privilege against self-incrimination is jeopardized. Procedural safeguards must be employed to protect the privilege and unless other fully effective means are adopted to notify the person of his right of silence and to assure that the exercise of the right will be scrupulously honored, the following measures are required. He must be warned prior to any questioning that he has the right to remain silent, that anything he says can be used against him in a court of law, that he has the right to the presence of an attorney, and that if he cannot afford an attorney one will be appointed for him prior to any questioning if he so desires. Opportunity to exercise these rights must be afforded to him throughout the interrogation. After such warnings have been given, and such opportunity afforded him, the individual may knowingly and intelligently waive these rights and agree to answer questions or make a statement. But unless and until such warnings and waiver are demonstrated by the prosecution at trial, no evidence obtained as a result of interrogation can be used against him.

* * * *

Decision

Reversed.

NEW YORK TIMES Co.
v.
UNITED STATES
403 U.S. 713, 91 S.Ct. 2140, 29 L.Ed.2d 822.
Argued June 26, 1971.
Decided June 30, 1971.

Introduction

A freedom of press/prior restraint case involving the publication of sensitive government documents relating to the government's policy in Vietnam from 1945 to 1967. The U.S. government attempted to suspend the publication of the so-called *Pentagon Papers*, but the Court held that the government could only prosecute after publication, not before.

WESTLAW Summary

The United States sought to enjoin newspapers from publishing contents of classified historical study on Viet Nam policy. In one case, the District Court for the Southern District of New York rendered judgment from which the Government appealed, and the Court of Appeals for the Second Circuit remanded and continued stay. In the other case, the District Court for the District of Columbia rendered judgment from which the Government appealed, and the Court of Appeals for the District of Columbia Circuit affirmed. In both cases certiorari was granted. The Supreme Court held that the Government had not met its burden of showing justification for the imposition of restraint on the publication of the contents of the study.

Case Excerpts

PER CURIAM.

We granted certiorari in these cases in which the United States seeks to enjoin the New York Times and the Washington Post from publishing the contents of a classified study entitled "History of U.S. Decision-Making Process on Viet Nam Policy."

"Any system of prior restraints of expression comes to this Court bearing a heavy presumption against its constitutional validity." The Government "thus carries a heavy burden of showing justification for the imposition of such a restraint." The District Court for the Southern District of New York in the New York Times case and the District Court for the District of Columbia and the Court of Appeals for the District of Columbia Circuit, in the Washington Post case, held that the Government had not met that burden. We agree.

The judgment of the Court of Appeals for the District of Columbia Circuit is therefore affirmed. The order of the Court of Appeals for the Second Circuit is reversed and the case is remanded with directions to enter a judgment affirming the judgment of the District Court for the Southern District of New York. The stays entered June 25, 1971, by the Court are vacated. The judgments shall issue forthwith.

So ordered.

Mr. Justice BLACK, with whom Mr. Justice DOUGLAS joins, concurring.

I adhere to the view that the Government's case against the Washington Post should have been dismissed and that the injunction against the New York Times should have been vacated without oral argument when the cases were first presented to this Court. I believe that every moment's continuance of the injunctions against these newspapers amounts to a flagrant, indefensible, and continuing violation of the First Amendment. Furthermore, after oral argument, I agree completely that we must affirm the judgment of the Court of Appeals for the District of Columbia Circuit and reverse the judgment of the Court of Appeals for the Second Circuit. * * *. In my view it is unfortunate that some of my Brethren are apparently willing to hold that the publication of news may sometimes be enjoined. Such a holding would make a shambles of the First Amendment.

Our Government was launched in 1789 with the adoption of the Constitution. The Bill of Rights, including the First Amendment, followed in 1791. Now, for the first time in the 182 years since the founding of the Republic, the federal courts are asked to hold that the First Amendment does not mean what it says, but rather means that the Government can halt the publication of current news of vital importance to the people of this country.

In seeking injunctions against these newspapers and in its presentation to the Court, the Executive Branch seems to have forgotten the essential purpose and history of the First Amendment. When the Constitution was adopted, many people strongly opposed it because the document contained no Bill of Rights to safeguard certain basic freedoms. They especially feared that the new powers granted to a central government might be interpreted to permit the government to curtail freedom of religion, press, assembly, and speech. In response to an overwhelming public clamor, James Madison offered a series of amendments to satisfy citizens that these great liberties would remain safe and beyond the power of government to abridge. Madison proposed what later became the First Amendment in three parts, two of which are set out below, and one of which proclaimed: "The people shall not be deprived or abridged of their right to speak, to write, or to publish their sentiments; and the freedom of the press, as one of the great bulwarks of liberty, shall be inviolable." The amendments were offered to curtail and restrict the general powers granted to the Executive, Legislative, and Judicial Branches two years before in the original Constitution. The Bill of Rights changed the original Constitution into a new charter under which no branch of government could abridge the people's freedoms of press, speech, religion, and assembly. Yet the Solicitor General argues and some members of the Court appear to agree that the general powers of the Government adopted in the original Constitution should be interpreted to limit and restrict the specific and emphatic guarantees of the Bill of Rights adopted later. I can imagine no greater perversion of history. Madison and the other Framers of the First Amendment, able men that they were, wrote in language they earnestly believed could never be misunderstood: "Congress shall make no law * * * abridging the freedom * * * of the press * * *." Both the history and language of the First Amendment support the view that the press must be left free to publish news, whatever the source, without censorship, injunctions, or prior restraints.

In the First Amendment the Founding Fathers gave the free press the protection it must have to fulfill its essential role in our democracy. The press was to serve the governed, not the governors. The Government's power to censor the press was abolished so that the press would remain forever free to censure the Government. The press was protected so that it could bare the secrets of government and inform the people. Only a free and unrestrained press can effectively expose deception in government. And paramount among the responsibilities of a free press is the duty to prevent any part of the government from deceiving the people and sending them off to distant lands to die of foreign fevers and foreign shot and shell. In my view, far from deserving condemnation for their courageous reporting, the New York Times, the Washington Post, and other newspapers should be commended for serving the purpose that the Founding Fathers saw so clearly. In revealing the workings of government that led to the Vietnam war, the newspapers nobly did precisely that which the Founders hoped and trusted they would do.

The Government's case here is based on premises entirely different from those that guided the Framers of the First Amendment. The Solicitor General has carefully and emphatically stated:

"Now, Mr. Justice (BLACK), your construction of * * * (the First Amendment) is well known, and I certainly respect it. You say that no law means no law, and that should be obvious. I can only say, Mr. Justice, that to me it is equally obvious that "no law" does not mean "no law," and I would seek to persuade the Court that that is true. * * * (T)here are other parts of the Constitution that grant powers and responsibilities to the Executive, and * * * the First Amendment was not intended to make it impossible for the Executive to function or to protect the security of the United States."

And the Government argues in its brief that in spite of the First Amendment, "(t)he authority of the Executive Department to protect the nation against publication of information whose disclosure would endanger the national security stems from two interrelated sources: the constitutional power of the President over the conduct of foreign affairs and his authority as Commander-in-Chief."

In other words, we are asked to hold that despite the First Amendment's emphatic command, the Executive Branch, the Congress, and the Judiciary can make laws enjoining publication of current news and abridging freedom of the press in the name of "national security." The Government does not even attempt to rely on any act of Congress. Instead it makes the bold and dangerously far-reaching contention that the courts should take it upon themselves to "make" a law abridging freedom of the press in the name of equity, presidential power and national security, even when the representatives of the people in Congress have adhered to the command of the First Amendment and refused to make such a law. To find that the President has "inherent power" to halt the publication of news by resort to the courts would wipe out the First Amendment and destroy the fundamental liberty and security of the very people the Government hopes to make "secure." No one can read the history of the adoption of the First Amendment without being convinced beyond any doubt that it was injunctions like those sought here that Madison and his collaborators intended to outlaw in this Nation for all time.

The word "security" is a broad, vague generality whose contours should not be invoked to abrogate the fundamental law embodied in the First Amendment. The guarding of military and diplomatic secrets at the expense of informed representative government provides no real security for our Republic. The Framers of the First Amendment, fully aware of both the need to defend a new nation and the abuses of the English and Colonial Governments, sought to give this new society strength and security by providing that freedom of speech, press, religion, and assembly should not be abridged. This thought was eloquently expressed in 1937 by Mr. Chief Justice Hughes—great man and great Chief Justice that he was—when the Court held a man could not be punished for attending a meeting run by Communists.

"The greater the importance of safeguarding the community from incitements to the overthrow of our institutions by force and violence, the more imperative is the need to preserve inviolate the constitutional rights of free speech, free press and free assembly in order to maintain the opportunity for free political discussion, to the end that government may be responsive to the will of the people and that changes, if desired, may be obtained by peaceful means. Therein lies the security of the Republic, the very foundation of constitutional government."

Decision

Judgment of the Court of Appeals for the District of Columbia Circuit affirmed; order of the Court of Appeals for the Second Circuit reversed and case remanded with directions.

PLESSY
v.
FERGUSON
163 U.S. 537, 16 S.Ct. 1138, 41, L.Ed. 256.
May 18, 1896.

Introduction

A Fourteenth Amendment case in which the Supreme Court upheld the constitutionality of an ordinance requiring blacks and whites to use separate railway accommodations.

WESTLAW Summary

[Not available.]

Case Excerpts

Mr. Justice BROWN * * * delivered the opinion of the court.

This case turns upon the constitutionality of an act of the general assembly of the state of Louisiana, passed in 1890, providing for separate railway carriages for the white and colored races.
* * * *
The information filed in the criminal district court charged, in substance, that Plessy, being a passenger between two stations within the state of Louisiana, was assigned by officers of the company to the coach used for the race to which he belonged, but he insisted upon going into a coach used by the race to which he did not belong. Neither in the information nor plea was his particular race or color averred.

The petition for the writ of prohibition averred that petitioner was seven-eights Caucasian and one-eighth African blood; that the mixture of colored blood was not discernible in him; and that he was entitled to every right, privilege, and immunity secured to citizens of the United States of the white race; and that, upon such theory, he took possession of a vacant seat in a coach where passengers of the white race were accommodated, and was ordered by the conductor to vacate said coach, and take a seat in another, assigned to persons of the colored race, and, having refused to comply with such demand, he was forcibly ejected, with the aid of a police officer, and imprisoned in the parish jail to answer a charge of having violated the above act.

The constitutionality of this act is attacked upon the ground that it conflicts both with the thirteenth amendment of the constitution, abolishing slavery, and the fourteenth amendment, which prohibits certain restrictive legislation on the part of the states.

That it does not conflict with the thirteenth amendment, which abolished slavery and involuntary servitude, except as a punishment for crime, is too clear for argument. * * *
* * * *

By the fourteenth amendment, all persons born or naturalized in the United States, and subject to the jurisdiction thereof, are made citizens of the United States and of the state wherein they reside; and the states are forbidden from making or enforcing any law which shall abridge the privileges or immunities of citizens of the United States, or shall deprive any person of life, liberty, or property without due process of law, or deny to any person within their jurisdiction the equal protection of the laws.
* * * *

The object of the [fourteenth] amendment was undoubtedly to enforce the absolute equality of the two races before the law, but, in the nature of things, it could not have been intended to abolish distinctions based upon color, or to enforce social, as distinguished from political, equality, or a commingling of the two races upon terms unsatisfactory to either. Laws permitting, and even requiring, their separation, in places where they are liable to be brought into contact, do not necessarily imply the inferiority of either race to the other, and have been generally, if not universally, recognized as within the competency of the state legislatures in the exercise of their police power. The most common instance of this is connected with the establishment of separate schools for white and colored children, which have been held to be a valid exercise of the legislative power even by courts of states where the political rights of the colored race have been longest and most earnestly enforced.

* * * *

* * * [It is] suggested by the learned counsel for the plaintiff in error that the same argument that will justify the state legislature in requiring railways to provide separate accommodations for the two races will also authorize them to require separate cars to be provided for people whose hair is of a certain color, or who are aliens, or who belong to certain nationalities, or to enact laws requiring colored people to walk upon one side of the street, and white people upon the other, or requiring white men's houses to be painted white, and colored men's black, or their vehicles or business signs to be of different colors, upon the theory that one side of the street is as good as the other, or that a house or vehicle of one color is as good as one of another color. The reply to all this is that every exercise of the police power must be reasonable, and extend only to such laws as are enacted in good faith for the promotion of the public good, and not for the annoyance or oppression of a particular class. * * *

So far, then, as a conflict with the fourteenth amendment is concerned, the case reduces itself to the question whether the statute of Louisiana is a reasonable regulation, and with respect to this there must necessarily be a large discretion on the part of the legislature. In determining the question of reasonableness, it is at liberty to act with reference to the established usages, customs, and traditions of the people, and with a view to the promotion of their comfort, and the preservation of the public peace and good order. Gauged by this standard, we cannot say that a law which authorizes or even requires the separation of the two races in public conveyances is unreasonable, or more obnoxious to the fourteenth amendment than the acts of congress requiring separate schools for colored children in the District of Columbia, the constitutionality of which does not seem to have been questioned, or the corresponding acts of state legislatures.

We consider the underlying fallacy of the plaintiff's argument to consist in the assumption that the enforced separation of the two races stamps the colored race with a badge of inferiority. If this be so, it is not by reason of anything found in the act, but solely because the colored race chooses to put that construction upon it. * * * The argument also assumes that social prejudices may be overcome by legislation, and that equal rights cannot be secured to the negro except by an enforced commingling of the two races. We cannot accept this proposition. If the two races are to meet upon terms of social equality, it must be the result of natural affinities, a mutual appreciation of each other's merits, and a voluntary consent of individuals. * * * Legislation is powerless to eradicate racial instincts, or to abolish distinctions based upon physical differences, and the attempt to do so can only result in accentuating the difficulties of the present situation. If the civil and political rights of both races be equal, one cannot be inferior to the other civilly or politically. If one race be inferior to the other socially, the constitution of the United States cannot put them upon the same plane.

It is true that the question of the proportion of colored blood necessary to constitute a colored person, as distinguished from a white person, is one upon which there is a difference of opinion in the different states; some holding that any visible admixture of black blood stamps the person as belonging to the colored race; and still others, that the predominance of white blood must only be in the proportion of three-fourths. But these are questions to be determined under the laws of each state, and are not properly put in issue in this case. * * *.

Decision

The judgment of the court below is therefore affirmed.

POWELL et al.

v.

State of **ALABAMA**

287 U.S. 45, 53 S.Ct. 55, 77 L.Ed. 158.

Argued Oct. 10, 1932.

Decided Nov. 7, 1932.

Introduction

A Sixth Amendment right to counsel case in which the Court ruled that the accused has a right to a lawyer in capital punishment cases.

WESTLAW Summary

Ozie Powell and two others, Haywood Patterson, and Charley Weems, were convicted of rape. The convictions were affirmed by the Supreme Court of Alabama and the defendants bring certiorari. The Supreme Court reversed the judgments and remanded the causes for further proceedings in accordance with the opinion.

Case Excerpts

Mr. Justice SUTHERLAND delivered the opinion of the Court.

These cases were argued together and submitted for decision as one case.

The petitioners, hereinafter referred to as defendants, are negroes charged with the crime of rape, committed upon the persons of two white girls. The crime is said to have been committed on March 25, 1931. The indictment was returned in a state court of first instance on March 31, and the record recites that on the same day the defendants were arraigned and entered pleas of not guilty. There is a further recital

132 HANDBOOK OF SELECTED COURT CASES

to the effect that upon the arraignment they were represented by counsel. But no counsel had been employed, and aside from a statement made by the trial judge several days later during a colloquy immediately preceding the trial, the record does not disclose when, or under what circumstances, an appointment of counsel was made, or who was appointed. During the colloquy referred to, the trial judge, in response to a question, said that he had appointed all the members of the bar for the purpose of arraigning the defendants and then of course anticipated that the members of the bar would continue to help the defendants if no counsel appeared. Upon the argument here both sides accepted that as a correct statement of the facts concerning the matter.

There was a severance upon the request of the state, and the defendants were tried in three several groups, as indicated above. As each of the three cases was called for trial, each defendant was arraigned, and, having the indictment read to him, entered a plea of not guilty. Whether the original arraignment and pleas were regarded as ineffective is not shown. Each of the three trials was completed within a single day. Under the Alabama statute the punishment for rape is to be fixed by the jury, and in its discretion may be from ten years imprisonment to death. The juries found defendants guilty and imposed the death penalty upon all. The trial court overruled motions for new trials and sentenced the defendants in accordance with the verdicts. The judgments were affirmed by the state supreme court. Chief Justice Anderson thought the defendants had not been accorded a fair trial and strongly dissented.

In this court the judgments are assailed upon the grounds that the defendants, and each of them, were denied due process of law and the equal protection of the laws, in contravention of the Fourteenth Amendment, specifically as follows: (1) They were not given a fair, impartial, and deliberate trial; (2) they were denied the right of counsel, with the accustomed incidents of consultation and opportunity of preparation for trial; and (3) they were tried before juries from which qualified members of their own race were systematically excluded. These questions were properly raised and saved in the courts below.

The only one of the assignments which we shall consider is the second, in respect of the denial of counsel; and it becomes unnecessary to discuss the facts of the case or the circumstances surrounding the prosecution except in so far as they reflect light upon that question.

The record shows that on the day when the offense is said to have been committed, these defendants, together with a number of other negroes, were upon a freight train on its way through Alabama. On the same train were seven white boys and the two white girls. A fight took place between the negroes and the white boys, in the course of which the white boys, with the exception of one named Gilley, were thrown off the train. A message was sent ahead, reporting the fight and asking that every negro be gotten off the train. The participants in the fight, and the two girls, were in an open gondola car. The two girls testified that each of them was assaulted by six different negroes in turn, and they identified the seven defendants as having been among the number. None of the white boys was called to testify, with the exception of Gilley, who was called in rebuttal.

Before the train reached Scottsboro, Ala., a sheriff's posse seized the defendants and two other negroes. Both girls and the negroes then were taken to Scottsboro, the county seat. Word of their coming and of the alleged assault had preceded them, and they were met at Scottsboro by a large crowd. It does not sufficiently appear that the defendants were seriously threatened with, or that they were actually in danger of, mob violence; but it does appear that the attitude of the community was one of great hostility. The sheriff thought it necessary to call for the militia to assist in safeguarding the prisoners. Chief Justice Anderson pointed out in his opinion that every step taken from the arrest and arraignment to the sentence was accompanied by the military. Soldiers took the defendants to Gadsden for safe-keeping, brought them back to Scottsboro for arraignment, returned them to Gadsden for safekeeping while awaiting trial, escorted them to Scottsboro for trial a few days later, and guarded the courthouse and grounds at every stage of the proceedings. It is perfectly apparent that the proceedings, from beginning to end, took place in an atmosphere of tense, hostile, and excited public sentiment. During the entire time, the defendants were closely confined or were under military guard. The record does not disclose their ages, except that one of them was nineteen; but the record clearly indicates that most, if not all, of them were youthful, and they are constantly referred to as "the boys." They were ignorant and illiterate. All of them were residents of other states, where alone members of their families or friends resided.

However guilty defendants, upon due inquiry, might prove to have been, they were, until convicted, presumed to be innocent. It was the duty of the court having their cases in charge to see that they were denied no necessary incident of a fair trial. With any error of the state court involving alleged contravention of the state statutes or Constitution we, of course, have nothing to do. The sole inquiry which we are permitted to make is whether the federal Constitution was contravened and as to that, we confine ourselves, as already suggested, to the inquiry whether the defendants were in substance denied the right of counsel, and if so, whether such denial infringes the due process clause of the Fourteenth Amendment.

* * * The record shows that immediately upon the return of the indictment defendants were arraigned and pleaded not guilty. Apparently they were not asked whether they had, or were able to employ, counsel, or wished to have counsel appointed; or whether they had friends or relatives who might assist in that regard if communicated with. * * *

It is hardly necessary to say that the right to counsel being conceded, a defendant should be afforded a fair opportunity to secure counsel of his own choice. Not only was that not done here, but such designation of counsel as was attempted was either so indefinite or so close upon the trial as to amount to a denial of effective and substantial aid in that regard. * * *

* * * *

It thus will be seen that until the very morning of the trial no lawyer had been named or definitely designated to represent the defendants. Prior to that time, the trial judge had "appointed all the members of the bar" for the limited "purpose of arraigning the defendants." Whether they would represent the defendants thereafter, if no counsel appeared in their behalf, was a matter of speculation only, or, as the judge indicated, of mere anticipation on the part of the court. Such a designation, even if made for all purposes, would, in our opinion, have fallen far short of meeting, in any proper sense, a requirement for the appointment of counsel. How many lawyers were members of the bar does not appear; but, in the very nature of things, whether many or few, they would not, thus collectively named, have been given that clear appreciation of responsibility or impressed with that individual sense of duty which should and naturally would accompany the appointment of a selected member of the bar, specifically named and assigned.

* * * *

It is not enough to assume that counsel thus precipitated into the case thought there was no defense, and exercised their best judgment in proceeding to trial without preparation. Neither they nor the court could say what a prompt and thoroughgoing investigation might disclose as to the facts. No attempt was made to investigate. No opportunity to do so was given. Defendants were immediately hurried to trial. Chief Justice Anderson, after disclaiming any intention to criticize harshly counsel who attempted to represent defendants at the trials, said: "* * * The record indicates that the appearance was rather pro forma than zealous and active * * *." Under the circumstances disclosed, we hold that defendants were not accorded the right of counsel in any substantial sense. * * *

* * * *

In the light of the facts outlined in the forepart of this opinion—the ignorance and illiteracy of the defendants, their youth, the circumstances of public hostility, the imprisonment and the close surveillance of the defendants by the military forces, the fact that their friends and families were all in other states and communication with them necessarily difficult, and above all that they stood in deadly peril of their lives—we think the failure of the trial court to give them reasonable time and opportunity to secure counsel was a clear denial of due process.

* * * *

The United States by statute and every state in the Union by express provision of law, or by the determination of its courts, make it the duty of the trial judge, where the accused is unable to employ counsel, to appoint counsel for him. In most states the rule applies broadly to all criminal prosecutions, in others it is limited to the more serious crimes, and in a very limited number, to capital cases. A rule adopted with such unanimous accord reflects, if it does not establish the inherent right to have counsel appointed at least in cases like the present, and lends convincing support to the conclusion we have reached as to the fundamental nature of that right.

Decision

The judgments must be reversed and the causes remanded for further proceedings not inconsistent with this opinion.

Jay **PRINTZ**, Sheriff/Coroner, Ravalli County, Montana
v.
UNITED STATES
521 U.S. 898, 117 S.Ct. 2365, 138 L.Ed.2d 914.
Supreme Court of the United States.
Argued Dec. 3, 1996.
Decided June 27, 1997.

Introduction

A state sovereignty case in which Congress was held to have violated constitutional principles by ordering state law enforcement officers to receive firearms' dealers' reports and conduct background checks as part of a federal program.

WESTLAW Summary

County sheriff sought to enjoin enforcement of provisions of Brady Handgun Violence Prevention Act imposing requirements on chief law enforcement officers (CLEO). The United States District Court for the District of Montana, Charles C. Lovell, J. [Judge], held background check requirement to be unconstitutional. Another county sheriff brought separate action to declare Brady Act unconstitutional. The United States District Court for the District of Arizona, John M. Roll, J. [Judge], found that background search requirement was unconstitutional. Parties appealed, and cases were consolidated. The Court of Appeals for the Ninth Circuit reversed. Certiorari was granted. The Supreme Court, Justice Scalia, held that: (1) obligation to conduct background checks on prospective handgun purchasers imposed unconstitutional obligation on state officers to execute federal laws; (2) sheriffs were not in position to challenge Act's requirements that CLEOs destroy handgun-applicant statements and give would-be purchasers written statements of reasons for determining their ineligibility to receive handguns; and (3) there were no plaintiffs before Court who could challenge provisions requiring firearms dealers to forward to CLEO notice of contents of handgun-applicant statement, and to wait five business days before consummating sale.

Case Excerpts

Justice SCALIA delivered the opinion of the Court.

* * * *

The Government observes that statutes enacted by the first Congresses required state courts to record applications for citizenship, to transmit abstracts of citizenship applications and other naturalization records to the Secretary of State, and to register aliens seeking naturalization and issue certificates of registry. It may well be, however, that these requirements applied only in States that authorized their courts to conduct naturalization proceedings. Other statutes of that era apparently or at least arguably required state courts to perform functions unrelated to naturalization, such as resolving controversies between a captain and the crew of his ship concerning the seaworthiness of the vessel, hearing the claims of slave owners who had apprehended fugitive slaves and issuing certificates authorizing the slave's forced removal to the State from which he had fled, taking proof of the claims of Canadian refugees who had assisted the United States during the Revolutionary War, and ordering the deportation of alien enemies in times of war.

These early laws establish, at most, that the Constitution was originally understood to permit imposition of an obligation on state judges to enforce federal prescriptions, insofar as those prescriptions related to matters appropriate for the judicial power. * * * It is understandable why courts should have been viewed distinctively in this regard; unlike legislatures and executives, they applied the law of other sovereigns all the time. The principle underlying so-called "transitory" causes of action was that laws which operated elsewhere created obligations in justice that courts of the forum state would enforce. The Constitution itself, in the Full Faith and Credit Clause, generally required such enforcement with respect to obligations arising in other

States. For these reasons, we do not think the early statutes imposing obligations on state courts imply a power of Congress to impress the state executive into its service. Indeed, it can be argued that the numerousness of these statutes, contrasted with the utter lack of statutes imposing obligations on the States' executive (notwithstanding the attractiveness of that course to Congress), suggests an assumed absence of such power. * * *

* * * *

* * * We turn next to consideration of the structure of the Constitution, to see if we can discern * * * a principle that controls the present cases.

* * * *

It is incontestible that the Constitution established a system of "dual sovereignty." Although the States surrendered many of their powers to the new Federal Government, they retained "a residuary and inviolable sovereignty." This is reflected throughout the Constitution's text * * * . Residual state sovereignty was also implicit, of course, in the Constitution's conferral upon Congress of not all governmental powers, but only discrete, enumerated ones, which implication was rendered express by the Tenth Amendment's assertion that "[t]he powers not delegated to the United States by the Constitution, nor prohibited by it to the States, are reserved to the States respectively, or to the people."

* * * *

This separation of the two spheres is one of the Constitution's structural protections of liberty. * * * The power of the Federal Government would be augmented immeasurably if it were able to impress into its service—and at no cost to itself—the police officers of the 50 States.

* * * *

* * * It would also have an effect upon * * * the separation and equilibration of powers between the three branches of the Federal Government itself. The Constitution does not leave to speculation who is to administer the laws enacted by Congress; the President, it says, "shall take Care that the Laws be faithfully executed," personally and through officers whom he appoints (save for such inferior officers as

Congress may authorize to be appointed by the "Courts of Law" or by "the Heads of Departments" who are themselves presidential appointees). The Brady Act effectively transfers this responsibility to thousands of CLEOs in the 50 States, who are left to implement the program without meaningful Presidential control (if indeed meaningful Presidential control is possible without the power to appoint and remove). The insistence of the Framers upon unity in the Federal Executive—to insure both vigor and accountability—is well known. That unity would be shattered, and the power of the President would be subject to reduction, if Congress could act as effectively without the President as with him, by simply requiring state officers to execute its laws.

* * * *

The Government contends that * * * the background-check provision of the Brady Act does not require state legislative or executive officials to make policy, but instead issues a final directive to state CLEOs. It is permissible, the Government asserts, for Congress to command state or local officials to assist in the implementation of federal law so long as "Congress itself devises a clear legislative solution that regulates private conduct" and requires state or local officers to provide only "limited, non-policymaking help in enforcing that law. * * * [T]he constitutional line is crossed only when Congress compels the States to make law in their sovereign capacities."

The Government's distinction between "making" law and merely "enforcing" it, between "policymaking" and mere "implementation," is an interesting one. It is perhaps not meant to be the same as, but it is surely reminiscent of, the line that separates proper congressional conferral of Executive power from unconstitutional delegation of legislative authority for federal separation-of-powers purposes. This Court has not been notably successful in describing the latter line * * *. We are doubtful that the new line the Government proposes would be any more distinct. Executive action that has utterly no policymaking component is rare, particularly at an executive level as high as a jurisdiction's chief law-enforcement officer. Is it really true that there is no policymaking involved in deciding, for example, what "reasonable efforts" shall be expended to conduct a background check? It may well satisfy the Act for a

CLEO to direct that (a) no background checks will be conducted that divert personnel time from pending felony investigations, and (b) no background check will be permitted to consume more than one-half hour of an officer's time. But nothing in the Act requires a CLEO to be so parsimonious; diverting at least some felony-investigation time, and permitting at least some background checks beyond one-half hour would certainly not be unreasonable. Is this decision whether to devote maximum "reasonable efforts" or minimum "reasonable efforts" not preeminently a matter of policy? It is quite impossible, in short, to draw the Government's proposed line at "no policymaking," and we would have to fall back upon a line of "not too much policymaking." How much is too much is not likely to be answered precisely; and an imprecise barrier against federal intrusion upon state authority is not likely to be an effective one.

Even assuming, moreover, that the Brady Act leaves no "policymaking" discretion with the States, we fail to see how that improves rather than worsens the intrusion upon state sovereignty. * * * It is an essential attribute of the States' retained sovereignty that they remain independent and autonomous within their proper sphere of authority. It is no more compatible with this independence and autonomy that their officers be "dragooned" into administering federal law, than it would be compatible with the independence and autonomy of the United States that its officers be impressed into service for the execution of state laws.

* * * *

* * * Congress cannot compel the States to enact or enforce a federal regulatory program. Today we hold that Congress cannot circumvent that prohibition by conscripting the State's officers directly. The Federal Government may neither issue directives requiring the States to address particular problems, nor command the States' officers, or those of their political subdivisions, to administer or enforce a federal regulatory program. * * * [S]uch commands are fundamentally incompatible with our constitutional system of dual sovereignty.

Decision

The Court reversed the decision of the court of appeals.

REGENTS OF THE UNIVERSITY OF CALIFORNIA
v.
Allan **BAKKE**
438 U.S. 265, 98 S.Ct. 2733, 57 L.Ed.2d 750.
Argued Oct. 12, 1977.
Decided June 28, 1978.

Introduction

A civil rights/reverse discrimination case in which the Court allowed the University of California Davis Campus Medical School to admit students on the bases of race if the school's aim is to combat the effects of past discriminations. The Court held, nonetheless, that Bakke must be admitted to the medical school because its admissions policy had used race as the *sole* criterion for a limited number of "minority" positions.

WESTLAW Summary

A white male whose application to state medical school was rejected brought an action challenging the legality of the school's special admissions program under which 16 of the 100 positions in the class were reserved for "disadvantaged" minority students. The school cross-claimed for a declaratory judgment that its program was legal. The trial court declared the program illegal but refused to order the school to admit the applicant. The California Supreme Court affirmed the finding that the program was illegal and ordered the student admitted. The school sought certiorari. The Supreme Court held that: (1) the special admissions program was illegal, but (2) race may be one of a number of factors considered by the school in passing on applications, and (3) since the school could not show that the white applicant would not have been admitted even in the absence of the special admissions program, the applicant was entitled to be admitted.

Case Excerpts

Mr. Justice POWELL announced the judgment of the Court.

* * * *

The Medical School of the University of California at Davis opened in 1968 with an entering class of 50 students. In 1971, the size of the entering class was increased to 100 students, a level at which it remains. No admissions program for disadvantaged or minority students existed when the school opened, and the first class contained three Asians but no blacks, no Mexican-Americans, and no American Indians. Over the next two years, the faculty devised a special admissions program to increase the representation of "disadvantaged" students in each Medical School class. The special program consisted of a separate admissions system operating in coordination with the regular admissions process.

* * * *

From the year of the increase in class size—1971—through 1974, the special program resulted in the admission of 21 black students, 30 Mexican-Americans, and 12 Asians, for a total of 63 minority students. Over the same period, the regular admissions program produced 1 black, 6 Mexican-Americans, 276 and 37 Asians, for a total of 44 minority students. Although disadvantaged whites applied to the special program in large numbers, none received an offer of admission through that process. Indeed, in 1974, at least, the special committee explicitly considered only "disadvantaged" special applicants who were members of one of the designated minority groups.

Allan Bakke is a white male who applied to the Davis Medical School in 1973 under the general admissions program * * *. Despite a strong benchmark score of 468 out of 500, Bakke was rejected. His application had come late in the year, and no applicants in the general admissions process with scores below 470 were accepted after Bakke's application was completed. There were four special admissions slots unfilled at that time however, for which Bakke was not considered. * * *

Bakke's 1974 application was completed early in the year. His student interviewer gave him an overall rating of 94, finding him "friendly, well tempered, conscientious and delightful to speak with." His faculty interviewer was, by coincidence, the same Dr. Lowrey to whom he had written in protest of the special admissions program. * * * Dr. Lowrey gave Bakke the lowest of his six ratings, an 86; his total was 549 out of 600. Again, Bakke's application was rejected. In neither year did the chairman of the admissions committee, Dr. Lowrey, exercise his discretion to place Bakke on the waiting list. In both years, applicants were admitted under the special program with grade point averages, MCAT scores, and benchmark scores significantly lower than Bakke's.

After the second rejection, Bakke filed the instant suit in the Superior Court of California. He sought mandatory, injunctive, and declaratory relief compelling his admission to the Medical School. * * * The University cross-complained for a declaration that its special admissions program was lawful. The trial court found that the special program operated as a racial quota, because minority applicants in the special program were rated only against one another. Declaring that the University could not take race into account in making admissions decisions, the trial court held the challenged program violative of the Federal Constitution, the State Constitution, and Title VI. The court refused to order Bakke's admission, however, holding that he had failed to carry his burden of proving that he would have been admitted but for the existence of the special program.

Bakke appealed from the portion of the trial court judgment denying him admission, and the University appealed from the decision that its special admissions program was unlawful and the order enjoining it from considering race in the processing of applications. The Supreme Court of California transferred the case directly from the trial court, "because of the importance of the issues involved." The California court accepted the findings of the trial court with respect to the University's program. Because the special admissions program involved a racial classification, the Supreme Court held itself bound to apply strict scrutiny. It then turned to the goals the University presented as justifying the special program. * * * Without passing on the state constitutional or the federal statutory grounds cited in the trial court's judgment, the California court held that the Equal Protection Clause of the Fourteenth Amendment required that "no applicant may be rejected because of his race, in favor of another who is less qualified, as measured by standards applied without regard to race."

* * * *

In this Court the parties neither briefed nor argued the applicability of Title VI of the Civil Rights Act of 1964. Rather, as had the California court, they focused exclusively upon the validity of the special admissions program under the Equal Protection Clause. * * *

* * * *

En route to this crucial battle over the scope of judicial review, the parties fight a sharp preliminary action over the proper characterization of the special admissions program. Petitioner prefers to view it as establishing a "goal" of minority representation in the Medical School. Respondent, echoing the courts below, labels it a racial quota.

This semantic distinction is beside the point: The special admissions program is undeniably a classification based on race and ethnic background. To the extent that there existed a pool of at least minimally qualified minority applicants to fill the 16 special admissions seats, white applicants could compete only for 84 seats in the entering class, rather than the 100 open to minority applicants. Whether this limitation is described as a quota or a goal, it is a line drawn on the basis of race and ethnic status.

The guarantees of the Fourteenth Amendment extend to all persons. Its language is explicit: "No State shall . . . deny to any person within its jurisdiction the equal protection of the laws." It is settled beyond question that the "rights created by the first section of the Fourteenth Amendment are, by its terms, guaranteed to the individual. The rights established are personal rights." The guarantee of equal protection cannot mean one thing when applied to one individual and

something else when applied to a person of another color. If both are not accorded the same protection, then it is not equal.
* * * *

Petitioner urges us to adopt for the first time a more restrictive view of the Equal Protection Clause and hold that discrimination against members of the white "majority" cannot be suspect if its purpose can be characterized as "benign." The clock of our liberties, however, cannot be turned back to 1868. * * * "The Fourteenth Amendment is not directed solely against discrimination due to a 'two-class theory'—that is, based upon differences between 'white' and Negro."

Once the artificial line of a "two-class theory" of the Fourteenth Amendment is put aside, the difficulties entailed in varying the level of judicial review according to a perceived "preferred" status of a particular racial or ethnic minority are intractable. The concepts of "majority" and "minority" necessarily reflect temporary arrangements and political judgments. As observed above, the white "majority" itself is composed of various minority groups, most of which can lay claim to a history of prior discrimination at the hands of the State and private individuals. Not all of these groups can receive preferential treatment and corresponding judicial tolerance of distinctions drawn in terms of race and nationality, for then the only "majority" left would be a new minority of white Anglo-Saxon Protestants. There is no principled basis for deciding which groups would merit "heightened judicial solicitude" and which would not. * * *
* * * *

In summary, it is evident that the Davis special admissions program involves the use of an explicit racial classification never before countenanced by this Court. It tells applicants who are not Negro, Asian, or Chicano that they are totally excluded from a specific percentage of the seats in an entering class. No matter how strong their qualifications, quantitative and extracurricular, including their own potential for contribution to educational diversity, they are never afforded the chance to compete with applicants from the preferred groups for the special admissions seats. At the same time, the preferred applicants have the opportunity to compete for every seat in the class.

In enjoining petitioner from ever considering the race of any applicant, however, the courts below failed to recognize that the State has a substantial interest that legitimately may be served by a properly devised admissions program involving the competitive consideration of race and ethnic origin. For this reason, so much of the California court's judgment as enjoins petitioner from any consideration of the race of any applicant must be reversed.

With respect to respondent's entitlement to an injunction directing his admission to the Medical School, petitioner has conceded that it could not carry its burden of proving that, but for the existence of its unlawful special admissions program, respondent still would not have been admitted. Hence, respondent is entitled to the injunction, and that portion of the judgment must be affirmed.

Decision

Affirmed in part and reversed in part.

B. A. **REYNOLDS**, et al.,
v.
M. O. **SIMS** et al.
377 U.S. 533, 84 S.Ct. 1362, 12 L.Ed.2d 506.
Argued Nov. 13, 1963.
Decided June 15, 1964.
Rehearing Denied Oct. 12, 1964.

Introduction

A Congressional reapportionment case in which the Court ruled that both chambers of a state legislature must be apportioned with equal populations in each district. This "one-person, one-vote" principle had already been applied to Congressional districts in *Wesberry v. Sanders*.

WESTLAW Summary

Alabama legislative apportionment cases. The three-judge United States District Court for the Middle District of Alabama issued its decision, and appeals were taken. The Supreme Court held that the existing and two legislatively proposed plans for the apportionment of seats in the two houses of the Alabama Legislature were invalid under the Equal Protection Clause because the apportionment was not based on population and was completely lacking in rationality.

Case Excerpts

Mr. Chief Justice WARREN delivered the opinion of the Court.

Involved in these cases are an appeal and two cross-appeals from a decision of the Federal District Court for the Middle District of Alabama holding invalid, under the Equal Protection Clause of the Federal

Constitution, the existing and two legislative proposed plans for the apportionment of seats in the two houses of the Alabama Legislature, and ordering into effect a temporary reapportionment plan comprised of parts of the proposed but judicially disapproved measures.

On August 26, 1961, the original plaintiffs, residents, taxpayers and voters of Jefferson County, Alabama, filed a complaint in the United States District Court for the Middle District of Alabama, in their own behalf and on behalf of all similarly situated Alabama voters, challenging the apportionment of the Alabama Legislature. * * * The complaint alleged a deprivation of rights under the Alabama Constitution and under the Equal Protection Clause of the Fourteenth Amendment, and asserted that the District Court had jurisdiction under provisions of the Civil Rights Act.

* * * *

Plaintiffs below alleged that the last apportionment of the Alabama Legislature was based on the 1900 federal census, despite the requirement of the State Constitution that the legislature be reapportioned decennially. They asserted that, since the population growth in the State from 1900 to 1960 had been uneven, Jefferson and other counties were now victims of serious discrimination with respect to the allocation of legislative representation. As a result of the failure of the legislature to reapportion itself, plaintiffs asserted, they were denied "equal suffrage in free and equal elections * * * and the equal protection of the laws" in violation of the Alabama Constitution and the Fourteenth Amendment to the Federal Constitution. * * *

* * * Under the existing provisions, applying 1960 census figures, only 25.1% of the State's total population resided in districts represented by a majority of the members of the Senate, and only 25.7% lived in counties which could elect a majority of the members of the House of Representatives. Population-variance ratios of up to about 41-to-1 existed in the Senate, and up to about 16-to-1 in the House. Bullock County, with a population of only 13,462, and Henry County, with a population of only 15,286, each were allocated two seats in the Alabama House, whereas Mobile County, with a population of 314,301, was given only three seats, and Jefferson County, with 634,864 people, had only

seven representatives. With respect to senatorial apportionment, since the pertinent Alabama constitutional provisions had been consistently construed as prohibiting the giving of more than one Senate seat to any one county, Jefferson County, with over 600,000 people, was given only one senator, as was Lowndes County, with a 1960 population of only 15,417, and Wilcox County, with only 18,739 people.

* * * *

Undeniably the Constitution of the United States protects the right of all qualified citizens to vote, in state as well as in federal elections. A consistent line of decisions by this Court in cases involving attempts to deny or restrict the right of suffrage has made this indelibly clear. It has been repeatedly recognized that all qualified voters have a constitutionally protected right to vote * * *.

* * * *

A predominant consideration in determining whether a State's legislative apportionment scheme constitutes an invidious discrimination violative of rights asserted under the Equal Protection Clause is that the rights allegedly impaired are individual and personal in nature. * * * While the result of a court decision in a state legislative apportionment controversy may be to require the restructuring of the geographical distribution of seats in a state legislature, the judicial focus must be concentrated upon ascertaining whether there has been any discrimination against certain of the State's citizens which constitutes an impermissible impairment of their constitutionally protected right to vote. * * * Especially since the right to exercise the franchise in a free and unimpaired manner is preservative of other basic civil and political rights, any alleged infringement of the right of citizens to vote must be carefully and meticulously scrutinized. * * *

Legislators represent people, not trees or acres. Legislators are elected by voters, not farms or cities or economic interests. As long as ours is a representative form of government, and our legislatures are those instruments of government elected directly by and directly representative of the people, the right to elect legislators in a free and unimpaired fashion is a bedrock of our political system. It could hardly be gainsaid that a constitutional claim had been asserted by an allegation that certain otherwise qualified voters had been entirely prohibited from voting for members of their state legislature. And, if a State should provide that the votes of citizens in one part of the State should be given two times, or five times, or 10 times the weight of votes of citizens in another part of the State, it could hardly be contended that the right to vote of those residing in the disfavored areas had not been effectively diluted. It would appear extraordinary to suggest that a State could be constitutionally permitted to enact a law providing that certain of the State's voters could vote two, five, or 10 times for their legislative representatives, while voters living elsewhere could vote only once. And it is inconceivable that a state law to the effect that, in counting votes for legislators, the votes of citizens in one part of the State would be multiplied by two, five, or 10, while the votes of persons in another area would be counted only at face value, could be constitutionally sustainable. Of course, the effect of state legislative districting schemes which give the same number of representatives to unequal numbers of constituents is identical. * * *

Logically, in a society ostensibly grounded on representative government, it would seem reasonable that a majority of the people of a State could elect a majority of that State's legislators. To conclude differently, and to sanction minority control of state legislative bodies, would appear to deny majority rights in a way that far surpasses any possible denial of minority rights that might otherwise be thought to result. Since legislatures are responsible for enacting laws by which all citizens are to be governed, they should be bodies which are collectively responsive to the popular will. And the concept of equal protection has been traditionally viewed as requiring the uniform treatment of persons standing in the same relation to the governmental action questioned or challenged. With respect to the allocation of legislative representation, all voters, as citizens of a State, stand in the same relation regardless of where they live. * * *

* * * *

We hold that, as a basic constitutional standard, the Equal Protection Clause requires that the seats in both houses of a bicameral state legislature must be apportioned on a population basis. Simply

stated, an individual's right to vote for state legislators is unconstitutionally impaired when its weight is in a substantial fashion diluted when compared with votes of citizens living on other parts of the State. * * *
* * * *

Since we find the so-called federal analogy inapposite to a consideration of the constitutional validity of state legislative apportionment schemes, we necessarily hold that the Equal Protection Clause requires both houses of a state legislature to be apportioned on a population basis. The right of a citizen to equal representation and to have his vote weighted equally with those of all other citizens in the election of members of one house of a bicameral state legislature would amount to little if States could effectively submerge the equal-population principle in the apportionment of seats in the other house. * * * In summary, we can perceive no constitutional difference, with respect to the geographical distribution of state legislative representation, between the two houses of a bicameral state legislature.
* * * *

We find, therefore, that the action taken by the District Court in this case, in ordering into effect a reapportionment of both houses of the Alabama Legislature for purposes of the 1962 primary and general elections, by using the best parts of the two proposed plans which it had found, as a whole, to be invalid, was an appropriate and well-considered exercise of judicial power. Admittedly, the lower court's ordered plan was intended only as a temporary and provisional measure and the District Court correctly indicated that the plan was invalid as a permanent apportionment. In retaining jurisdiction while deferring a hearing on the issuance of a final injunction in order to give the provisionally reapportioned legislature an opportunity to act effectively, the court below proceeded in a proper fashion. Since the District Court evinced its realization that its ordered reapportionment could not be sustained as the basis for conducting the 1966 election of Alabama legislators, and avowedly intends to take some further action should the reapportioned Alabama Legislature fail to enact a constitutionally valid, permanent apportionment scheme in the interim, we affirm the judgment below and remand the cases for further proceedings consistent with the views stated in this opinion. It is so ordered.

Decision

Affirmed and remanded.

Jane **ROE**, et al.
v.
Henry **WADE**
410 U.S. 113, 93 S.Ct. 705, 35 L.Ed.2d 147.
Argued Dec. 13, 1971.
Reargued Oct. 11, 1972.
Decided Jan. 22, 1973.
Rehearing Denied Feb. 26, 1973.

Introduction

A privacy case in which the Court ruled that state anti-abortion laws were unconstitutional except when they applied to the last three months of pregnancy.

WESTLAW Summary

Action was brought for declaratory and injunctive relief respecting Texas criminal abortion laws which were claimed to be unconstitutional. A three-judge United States District Court for the Northern District of Texas entered judgment declaring the laws to be unconstitutional and an appeal was taken. The Supreme Court held that the Texas criminal abortion statutes prohibiting abortions at any stage of a pregnancy except to save the life of the mother are unconstitutional; that prior to approximately the end of the first trimester the abortion decision and its effectuation must be left to the medical judgment of the pregnant woman's attending physician, subsequent to approximately the end of the first trimester the state may regulate the abortion procedure in ways reasonably related to maternal health, and at the stage subsequent to viability the state may regulate and even proscribe abortion except where necessary in appropriate medical judgment for the preservation of the life or health of the mother.

Case Excerpts

Mr. Justice BLACKMUN delivered the opinion of the Court.

This Texas federal appeal and its Georgia companion, *Doe v. Bolton*, present constitutional challenges to state criminal abortion legislation. The Texas statutes under attack here are typical of those that have been in effect in many States for approximately a century. The Georgia statutes, in contrast, have a modern cast and are a legislative product that, to an extent at least, obviously reflects the influences of recent attitudinal changes, of advancing medical knowledge and techniques, and of new thinking about an old issue.

* * * *

The Texas statutes that concern us here are Art[icles] 1191-1194 and 1196 of the State's Penal Code. These make it a crime to "procure an abortion," as therein defined, or to attempt one, except with respect to "an abortion procured or attempted by medical advice for the purpose of saving the life of the mother." Similar statutes are in existence in a majority of the States. * * *

Jane Roe, a single woman who was residing in Dallas County, Texas, instituted this federal action in March 1970 against the District Attorney of the county. She sought a declaratory judgment that the Texas criminal abortion statutes were unconstitutional on their face, and an injunction restraining the defendant from enforcing the statutes.

Roe alleged that she was unmarried and pregnant; that she wished to terminate her pregnancy by an abortion "performed by a competent, licensed physician, under safe, clinical conditions"; that she was unable to get a "legal" abortion in Texas because her life did not appear to be threatened by the continuation of her pregnancy; and that she could not afford to travel to another jurisdiction in order to secure a legal abortion under safe conditions. She claimed that the Texas statutes were unconstitutionally vague and that they abridged her right of personal privacy, protected by the First, Fourth, Fifth, Ninth, and Fourteenth Amendments. By an amendment to her complaint Roe purported to sue "on behalf of herself and all other women" similarly situated.

* * * *

Viewing Roe's case as of the time of its filing and thereafter until as late as May, there can be little dispute that it then presented a case or controversy and that, wholly apart from the class aspects, she, as a pregnant single woman thwarted by the Texas criminal abortion laws, had standing to challenge those statutes. * * *

* * * *

The usual rule in federal cases is that an actual controversy must exist at stages of appellate or certiorari review, and not simply at the date the action is initiated. * * *

But when, as here, pregnancy is a significant fact in the litigation, the normal 266-day human gestation period is so short that the pregnancy will come to term before the usual appellate process is complete. If that termination makes a case moot, pregnancy litigation seldom will survive much beyond the trial stage, and appellate review will be effectively denied. Our law should not be that rigid. Pregnancy often comes more than once to the same woman, and in the general population, if man is to survive, it will always be with us. Pregnancy provides a classic justification for a conclusion of nonmootness. It truly could be "capable of repetition, yet evading review."

We, therefore, agree with the District Court that Jane Roe had standing to undertake this litigation, that she presented a justiciable controversy, and that the termination of her 1970 pregnancy has not rendered her case moot.

* * * *

The principal thrust of appellant's attack on the Texas statutes is that they improperly invade a right, said to be possessed by the pregnant woman, to choose to terminate her pregnancy. Appellant would discover this right in the concept of personal "liberty" embodied in the Fourteenth Amendment's Due Process Clause; or in personal marital, familial, and sexual privacy said to be protected by the Bill of Rights * * *.

* * * *

It has been argued occasionally that these laws were the product of a Victorian social concern to discourage illicit sexual conduct. * * *

A second reason is concerned with abortion as a medical procedure. When most criminal abortion laws were first enacted, the procedure was a hazardous one for the woman. * * *

* * * Mortality rates for women undergoing early abortions, where the procedure is legal, appear to be as low as or lower than the rates for normal childbirth. Consequently, any interest of the State in protecting the woman from an inherently hazardous procedure, except when it would be equally dangerous for her to forgo it, has largely disappeared. * * *

The third reason is the State's interest—some phrase it in terms of duty—in protecting prenatal life. Some of the argument for this justification rests on the theory that a new human life is present from the moment of conception. * * *

The Constitution does not explicitly mention any right of privacy. In a line of decisions, however, the Court has recognized that a right of personal privacy, or a guarantee of certain areas or zones of privacy, does exist under the Constitution. * * *

This right of privacy, whether it be founded in the Fourteenth Amendment's concept of personal liberty and restrictions upon state action, as we feel it is, or, as the District Court determined, in the Ninth Amendment's reservation of rights to the people, is broad enough to encompass a woman's decision whether or not to terminate her pregnancy. The detriment that the State would impose upon the pregnant woman by denying this choice altogether is apparent. Specific and direct harm medically diagnosable even in early pregnancy may be involved. Maternity, or additional offspring, may force upon the woman a distressful life and future. Psychological harm may be imminent. Mental and physical health may be taxed by child care. There is also the distress, for all concerned, associated with the unwanted child, and there is the problem of bringing a child into a family already unable, psychologically and otherwise, to care for it. In other cases, as in this one, the additional difficulties and continuing stigma of unwed motherhood may be involved. All these are factors the woman and her responsible physician necessarily will consider in consultation.

On the basis of elements such as these, appellant and some amice argue that the woman's right is absolute and that she is entitled to terminate her pregnancy at whatever time, in whatever way, and for whatever reason she alone chooses. With this we do not agree. Appellant's arguments that Texas either has no valid interest at all in regulating the abortion decision, or no interest strong enough to support any limitation upon the woman's sole determination, are unpersuasive. The Court's decisions recognizing a right of privacy also acknowledge that some state regulation in areas protected by that right is appropriate. As noted above, a State may properly assert important interests in safeguarding health, in maintaining medical standards, and in protecting potential life. At some point in pregnancy, these respective interests become sufficiently compelling to sustain regulation of the factors that govern the abortion decision. The privacy right involved, therefore, cannot be said to be absolute. In fact, it is not clear to us that the claim asserted by some amice that one has an unlimited right to do with one's body as one pleases bears a close relationship to the right of privacy previously articulated in the Court's decisions. * * *

We, therefore, conclude that the right of personal privacy includes the abortion decision, but that this right is not unqualified and must be considered against important state interests in regulation.

* * * *

* * * We repeat, however, that the State does have an important and legitimate interest in preserving and protecting the health of the pregnant woman, whether she be a resident of the State or a nonresident who seeks medical consultation and treatment there, and that it has still another important and legitimate interest in protecting the potentiality of human life. These interests are separate and distinct. Each grows in substantiality as the woman approaches term and, at a point during pregnancy, each becomes "compelling."

With respect to the State's important and legitimate interest in the health of the mother, the "compelling" point, in the light of present medical knowledge, is at approximately the end of the first trimester. This is so because of the now-established medical fact that until the end of the first trimester mortality in abortion may be less than mortality in normal childbirth. It follows that, from and after this point, a State may regulate the abortion procedure to the extent that the regulation reasonably relates to the preservation and protection of maternal health. * * *

This means, on the other hand, that, for the period of pregnancy prior to this "compelling" point, the attending physician, in consultation with his patient, is free to determine, without regulation by the State, that, in his medical judgment, the patient's pregnancy should be terminated. If that decision is reached, the judgment may be effectuated by an abortion free of interference by the State.

With respect to the State's important and legitimate interest in potential life, the "compelling" point is at viability. This is so because the fetus then presumably has the capability of meaningful life outside the mother's womb. State regulation protective of fetal life after viability thus has both logical and biological justifications. If the State is interested in protecting fetal life after viability, it may go so far as to proscribe abortion during that period, except when it is necessary to preserve the life or health of the mother.

Measured against these standards, Art[icle] 1196 of the Texas Penal Code, in restricting legal abortions to those "procured or attempted by medical advice for the purpose of saving the life of the mother," sweeps too broadly. The statute makes no distinction between abortions performed early in pregnancy and those performed later, and it limits to a single reason, "saving" the mother's life, the legal justification for the procedure. The statute, therefore, cannot survive the constitutional attack made upon it here.

* * * *

Decision

Affirmed in part and reversed in part.

Roy **ROMER,** Governor of Colorado, et al.
v.
Richard G. **EVANS** et al.
517 U.S. 620, 116 S.Ct. 1620, 134 L.Ed.2d 855.
Argued Oct. 10, 1995.
Decided May 20, 1996.

Introduction

A case challenging a Colorado constitutional amendment that prohibited any government unit from enacting laws or ordinances protecting the rights of gay males and lesbians. The Court held that the amendment violated the Fourteenth Amendment's guarantee of equal protection of the laws.

WESTLAW Summary

Homosexual persons, municipalities, and others brought action against governor, state attorney general, and state, challenging validity of amendment to Colorado Constitution that prohibited all legislative, executive, or judicial action designed to protect homosexual persons from discrimination. The District Court, City and County of Denver, H. Jeffrey Bayless, J., entered permanent injunction enjoining enforcement of amendment, and defendants appealed. The Colorado Supreme Court affirmed, and certiorari was granted. The Supreme Court, Justice Kennedy, held that amendment violated equal protection clause.

Case Excerpts

Justice KENNEDY delivered the opinion of the Court.

One century ago, the first Justice Harlan [in his dissent in *Plessy v. Ferguson*] admonished this Court that the Constitution "neither knows nor tolerates classes among citizens." Unheeded then, those words now are understood to state a commitment to the law's neutrality where the rights of persons are at stake. The Equal Protection Clause enforces this principle and today requires us to hold invalid a provision of Colorado's Constitution.

The enactment challenged in this case is an amendment to the Constitution of the State of Colorado, adopted in a 1992 statewide referendum. The parties and the state courts refer to it as "Amendment 2," its designation when submitted to the voters. The impetus for the amendment and the contentious campaign that preceded its adoption came in large part from ordinances that had been passed in various Colorado municipalities. For example, the cities of Aspen and Boulder and the City and County of Denver each had enacted ordinances which banned discrimination in many transactions and activities, including housing, employment, education, public accommodations, and health and welfare services. What gave rise to the statewide controversy was the protection the ordinances afforded to persons discriminated against by reason of their sexual orientation.

Yet Amendment 2, in explicit terms, does more than repeal or rescind these provisions. It prohibits all legislative, executive or judicial action at any level of state or local government designed to protect the named class, a class we shall refer to as homosexual persons or gays and lesbians. The amendment reads: "No Protected Status Based on Homosexual, Lesbian, or Bisexual Orientation. Neither the State of Colorado, through any of its branches or departments, nor any of its agencies, political subdivisions, municipalities or school districts, shall enact, adopt or enforce any statute, regulation, ordinance or policy whereby homosexual, lesbian or bisexual orientation, conduct, practices or relationships shall constitute or otherwise be the basis of or entitle any person or class of persons to have or claim any minority status, quota preferences, protected status or claim of discrimination. This Section of the Constitution shall be in all respects self-executing."

Soon after Amendment 2 was adopted, this litigation to declare its invalidity and enjoin its enforcement was commenced in the District Court for the City and County of Denver. * * *

The trial court granted a preliminary injunction to stay [suspend] enforcement of Amendment 2, and an appeal was taken to the Supreme

Court of Colorado. Sustaining the interim injunction and remanding the case for further proceedings, the State Supreme Court held that Amendment 2 was subject to strict scrutiny under the Fourteenth Amendment because it infringed the fundamental right of gays and lesbians to participate in the political process. On remand, the State advanced various arguments in an effort to show that Amendment 2 was narrowly tailored to serve compelling interests, but the trial court found none sufficient. It enjoined enforcement of Amendment 2, and the Supreme Court of Colorado, in a second opinion, affirmed the ruling. We granted certiorari * * *.

The State's principal argument in defense of Amendment 2 is that it puts gays and lesbians in the same position as all other persons. So, the State says, the measure does no more than deny homosexuals special rights. This reading of the amendment's language is implausible. We rely not upon our own interpretation of the amendment but upon the authoritative construction of Colorado's Supreme Court. The state court, deeming it unnecessary to determine the full extent of the amendment's reach, found it invalid even on a modest reading of its implications. The critical discussion of the amendment is as follows: "The immediate objective of Amendment 2 is, at a minimum, to repeal existing statutes, regulations, ordinances, and policies of state and local entities that barred discrimination based on sexual orientation.

"The 'ultimate effect' of Amendment 2 is to prohibit any governmental entity from adopting similar, or more protective statutes, regulations, ordinances, or policies in the future unless the state constitution is first amended to permit such measures."

Sweeping and comprehensive is the change in legal status effected by this law. So much is evident from the ordinances that the Colorado Supreme Court declared would be void by operation of Amendment 2. Homosexuals, by state decree, are put in a solitary class with respect to transactions and relations in both the private and governmental spheres. The amendment withdraws from homosexuals, but no others, specific legal protection from the injuries caused by discrimination, and it forbids reinstatement of these laws and policies.

* * * *

Amendment 2's reach may not be limited to specific laws passed for the benefit of gays and lesbians. It is a fair, if not necessary, inference from the broad language of the amendment that it deprives gays and lesbians even of the protection of general laws and policies that prohibit arbitrary discrimination in governmental and private settings. * * *

* * * *

The Fourteenth Amendment's promise that no person shall be denied the equal protection of the laws must co-exist with the practical necessity that most legislation classifies for one purpose or another, with resulting disadvantage to various groups or persons. We have attempted to reconcile the principle with the reality by stating that, if a law neither burdens a fundamental right nor targets a suspect class, we will uphold the legislative classification so long as it bears a rational relation to some legitimate end.

Amendment 2 fails, indeed defies, even this conventional inquiry. First, the amendment has the peculiar property of imposing a broad and undifferentiated disability on a single named group, an exceptional and, as we shall explain, invalid form of legislation. Second, its sheer breadth is so discontinuous with the reasons offered for it that the amendment seems inexplicable by anything but animus toward the class that it affects; it lacks a rational relationship to legitimate state interests.

Taking the first point, even in the ordinary equal protection case calling for the most deferential of standards, we insist on knowing the relation between the classification adopted and the object to be attained. The search for the link between classification and objective gives substance to the Equal Protection Clause; it provides guidance and discipline for the legislature, which is entitled to know what sorts of laws it can pass; and it marks the limits of our own authority. In the ordinary case, a law will be sustained if it can be said to advance a legitimate government interest, even if the law seems unwise or works to the disadvantage of a particular group, or if the rationale for it seems tenuous. The laws challenged in [previous cases cited by the Court] were narrow enough in scope and grounded in a sufficient factual context for us to ascertain that there existed some relation between the classification and the purpose it served. By requiring that the classification bear a rational relationship to an independent and legitimate legislative end, we ensure that classifications are not drawn for the purpose of disadvantaging the group burdened by the law.

Amendment 2 confounds this normal process of judicial review. It is at once too narrow and too broad. It identifies persons by a single trait and then denies them protection across the board. The resulting disqualification of a class of persons from the right to seek specific protection from the law is unprecedented in our jurisprudence. * * * It is not within our constitutional tradition to enact laws of this sort. Central both to the idea of the rule of law and to our own Constitution's guarantee of equal protection is the principle that government and each of its parts remain open on impartial terms to all who seek its assistance. Respect for this principle explains why laws singling out a certain class of citizens for disfavored legal status or general hardships are rare. A law declaring that in general it shall be more difficult for one group of citizens than for all others to seek aid from the government is itself a denial of equal protection of the laws in the most literal sense.

* * * *

A second and related point is that laws of the kind now before us raise the inevitable inference that the disadvantage imposed is born of animosity toward the class of persons affected. "[I]f the constitutional conception of 'equal protection of the laws' means anything, it must at the very least mean that a bare ... desire to harm a politically unpopular group cannot constitute a legitimate governmental interest." Even laws enacted for broad and ambitious purposes often can be explained by reference to legitimate public policies which justify the incidental disadvantages they impose on certain persons. Amendment 2, however, in making a general announcement that gays and lesbians shall not have any particular protections from the law, inflicts on them immediate, continuing, and real injuries that outrun and belie any legitimate justifications that may be claimed for it. We conclude that, in addition to the far-reaching deficiencies of Amendment 2 that we have noted, the principles it offends, in another sense, are conventional and venerable; a law must bear a rational relationship to a legitimate governmental purpose, and Amendment 2 does not.

The primary rationale the State offers for Amendment 2 is respect for other citizens' freedom of association, and in particular the liberties of landlords or employers who have personal or religious objections to homosexuality. Colorado also cites its interest in conserving resources to fight discrimination against other groups. The breadth of the Amendment is so far removed from these particular justifications that we find it impossible to credit them. We cannot say that Amendment 2 is directed to any identifiable legitimate purpose or discrete objective. It is a status-based enactment divorced from any factual context from which we could discern a relationship to legitimate state interests; it is a classification of persons undertaken for its own sake, something the Equal Protection Clause does not permit. "[C]lass legislation ... [is] obnoxious to the prohibitions of the Fourteenth Amendment...."

We must conclude that Amendment 2 classifies homosexuals not to further a proper legislative end but to make them unequal to everyone else. This Colorado cannot do. A State cannot so deem a class of persons a stranger to its laws.

Decision

Amendment 2 violates the Equal Protection Clause, and the judgment of the Supreme Court of Colorado is affirmed.

Chris **SALE**, Acting Commissioner, Immigration and Naturalization Service, et al., Petitioners
v.
HAITIAN CENTERS COUNCIL, INC., et al.
509 U.S. 155, 113 S.Ct. 2549, 125 L.Ed.2d 128.
Argued March 2, 1993.
Decided June 21, 1993.

Introduction

In 1981, President Ronald Reagan ordered the Coast Guard to intercept, outside the territorial waters of the United States, "vessels illegally transporting passengers from Haiti to the United States and return them to Haiti." After a military coup in Haiti in 1991, the United States feared that Haitian refugees would flood American shores much as Cuban refugees had done as a result of the communists' takeover of Cuba thirty years earlier. President George Bush issued Executive Order No. 12807, authorizing the Coast Guard to continue the forced repatriations. President Bill Clinton chose not to modify the order. The Supreme Court held that the presidents' order did not exceed their authority.

WESTLAW Summary

Action was brought by various organizations and Haitian aliens challenging procedures under an interdiction program with respect to Haitians fleeing Haiti. The United States District Court, Eastern District of New York, granted a preliminary injunction, and appeal was taken. The Second Circuit Court of Appeals modified and affirmed. Subsequently, the District Court denied plaintiffs' motion for a preliminary injunction prohibiting the government from returning interdicted Haitians, and the plaintiffs appealed. The Court of Appeals reversed. Certiorari was granted. The Supreme Court held that neither the statute generally prohibiting the Attorney General from deporting or returning aliens to a country where their life or freedom would be threatened on account of their race, religion, nationality, membership in a particular social group, or political opinion, nor a parallel article of the United Nations Convention Relating to Status of Refugees applied to actions taken by Coast Guard on high seas.

Case Excerpts

Justice STEVENS delivered the opinion of the Court.

* * * The question presented in this case is whether such forced repatriation, "authorized to be undertaken only beyond the territorial sea of the United States," violates [Section] 243(h)(1) of the Immigration and Nationality Act of 1952 (INA or Act) [or Article 33 of the United Nations Protocol Relating to the Status of Refugees].

* * * *

Aliens residing illegally in the United States are subject to deportation after a formal hearing. Aliens arriving at the border, or those who are temporarily paroled into the country, are subject to an exclusion hearing, the less formal process by which they, too, may eventually be removed from the United States. In either a deportation or exclusion proceeding the alien may seek asylum as a political refugee for whom removal to a particular country may threaten his life or freedom. Requests that the Attorney General grant asylum or withhold deportation to a particular country are typically, but not necessarily, advanced as parallel claims in either a deportation or an exclusion proceeding. When an alien proves that he is a "refugee," the Attorney General has discretion to grant him asylum * * *. If the proof shows that it is more likely than not that the alien's life or freedom would be threatened in a particular country because of his political or religious beliefs, under [Section] 243(h) the Attorney General must not send him to that country. The INA offers these statutory protections only to aliens who reside in or have arrived at the border of the United States. For 12 years, in one form or another, the interdiction program challenged here has prevented

Haitians such as respondents from reaching our shores and invoking those protections.

* * * *

In the ensuing decade, the Coast Guard interdicted approximately 25,000 Haitian migrants. After interviews conducted on board Coast Guard cutters, aliens who were identified as economic migrants were "screened out" and promptly repatriated. Those who made a credible showing of political refugee status were "screened in" and transported to the United States to file formal applications for asylum.

On September 30, 1991, a group of military leaders displaced the government of Jean Bertrand Aristide, the first democratically elected president in Haitian history. * * * [S]ince the military coup "hundreds of Haitians have been killed, tortured, detained without a warrant, or subjected to violence and the destruction of their property because of their political beliefs. Thousands have been forced into hiding." Following the coup the Coast Guard suspended repatriations for a period of several weeks, and the United States imposed economic sanctions on Haiti.

* * * *

* * * [T]he Haitian exodus expanded dramatically. During the six months after October 1991, the Coast Guard interdicted over 34,000 Haitians. Because so many interdicted Haitians could not be safely processed on Coast Guard cutters, the Department of Defense established temporary facilities at the United States Naval Base in Guantanamo, Cuba, to accommodate them during the screening process. Those temporary facilities, however, had a capacity of only about 12,500 persons. In the first three weeks of May 1992, the Coast Guard intercepted 127 vessels (many of which were considered unseaworthy, overcrowded, and unsafe); those vessels carried 10,497 undocumented aliens.

On May 22, 1992, the United States Navy determined that no additional migrants could safely be accommodated at Guantanamo.

With both the facilities at Guantanamo and available Coast Guard cutters saturated, and with the number of Haitian emigrants in unseaworthy craft increasing (many had drowned as they attempted the trip to Florida), the Government could no longer both protect our borders and offer the Haitians even a modified screening process. It had to choose between allowing Haitians into the United States for the screening process or repatriating them without giving them any opportunity to establish their qualifications as refugees. In the judgment of the President's advisors, the first choice not only would have defeated the original purpose of the program (controlling illegal immigration), but also would have impeded diplomatic efforts to restore democratic government in Haiti and would have posed a life-threatening danger to thousands of persons embarking on long voyages in dangerous craft. The second choice would have advanced those policies but deprived the fleeing Haitians of any screening process at a time when a significant minority of them were being screened in.

On May 23, 1992, President Bush adopted the second choice [and issued Executive Order No. 12807]. After assuming office, President Clinton decided not to modify that order; it remains in effect today.
* * *

* * * *

Respondents filed this lawsuit in the United States District Court for the Eastern District of New York on March 18, 1992 * * *. The plaintiffs include organizations that represent interdicted Haitians as well as Haitians who were then being detained at Guantanamo. They sued the Commissioner of the Immigration and Naturalization Service, the Attorney General, the Secretary of State, the Commandant of the Coast Guard, and the Commander of the Guantanamo Naval Base, complaining that the screening procedures provided on Coast Guard cutters and at

Guantanamo did not adequately protect their statutory and treaty rights to apply for refugee status and avoid repatriation to Haiti.

They alleged that the September 1991 coup had "triggered a continuing widely publicized reign of terror in Haiti"; that over 1,500 Haitians were believed to "have been killed or subjected to violence and destruction of their property because of their political beliefs and affiliations"; and that thousands of Haitian refugees "have set out in small boats that are often overloaded, unseaworthy, lacking basic safety equipment, and operated by inexperienced persons, braving the hazards of a prolonged journey over high seas in search of safety and freedom."

* * * *

Both parties argue that the plain language of [Section] 243(h)(1) is dispositive. It reads as follows: "The Attorney General shall not deport or return any alien (other than an alien described in section 1251(a)(4)(D) of this title) to a country if the Attorney General determines that such alien's life or freedom would be threatened in such country on account of race, religion, nationality, membership in a particular social group, or political opinion." * * *

* * * *

* * * [Section] 243(h)(1) refers only to the Attorney General * * *.

Other provisions of the Act expressly confer certain responsibilities on the Secretary of State, the President, and, indeed, on certain other officers as well. * * * We cannot say that the interdiction program created by the President, which the Coast Guard was ordered to enforce, usurped authority that Congress had delegated to, or implicated responsibilities that it had imposed on, the Attorney General alone.

The reference to the Attorney General in the statutory text is significant not only because that term cannot reasonably be construed to describe either the President or the Coast Guard, but also because it suggests that it applies only to the Attorney General's normal responsibilities under the INA. The most relevant of those responsibilities for our purposes is her conduct of the deportation and exclusion hearings in which requests for asylum or for withholding of deportation under [Section] 243(h) are ordinarily advanced. Since there is no provision in the statute for the conduct of such proceedings outside the United States, and since Part V and other provisions of the INA obviously contemplate that such proceedings would be held in the country, we cannot reasonably construe [Section] 243(h) to limit the Attorney General's actions in geographic areas where she has not been authorized to conduct such proceedings. Part V of the INA contains no reference to a possible extraterritorial application.

Even if Part V of the Act were not limited to strictly domestic procedures, the presumption that Acts of Congress do not ordinarily apply outside our borders would support an interpretation of [Section] 243(h) as applying only within United States territory. * * *

* * * *

In sum, all available evidence about the meaning of [Section] 243(h)--the government official at whom it is directed, its location in the Act, its failure to suggest any extraterritorial application, [and other evidence]--leads unerringly to the conclusion that it applies in only one context: the domestic procedures by which the Attorney General determines whether deportable and excludable aliens may remain in the United States.

* * * *

Like the text and the history of [Section] 243(h), the text and negotiating history of Article 33 of the United Nations Convention are both completely silent with respect to the Article's possible application to actions taken by a country outside its own borders. * * * [B]oth the text and negotiating history of Article 33 affirmatively indicate that it was not intended to have extraterritorial effect.

* * * *

It is perfectly clear that 8 U.S.C. [Section] 1182(f) grants the President ample power to establish a naval blockade that would simply deny illegal Haitian migrants the ability to disembark on our shores. Whether the President's chosen method of preventing the "attempted mass migration" of thousands of Haitians * * * poses a greater risk of harm to Haitians who might otherwise face a long and dangerous return voyage, is irrelevant to the scope of his authority to take action that neither the Convention nor the statute clearly prohibits. As we have already noted, Acts of Congress normally do not have extraterritorial application unless such an intent is clearly manifested. That presumption has special force when we are construing treaty and statutory provisions that may involve foreign and military affairs for which the President has unique responsibility. We therefore find ourselves in agreement with the conclusion expressed in [another case]: "This case presents a painfully common situation in which desperate people, convinced that they can no longer remain in their homeland, take desperate measures to escape. Although the human crisis is compelling, there is no solution to be found in a judicial remedy."

Decision

Reversed.

SMITH
v.
ALLWRIGHT
321 U.S. 649, 64 S.Ct. 657, 88 L.Ed. 987.
Reargued Jan. 12, 1944.
Decided April 3, 1944.
As Amended June 12, 1944.
Rehearing Denied May 8, 1944.

Introduction

A voting rights case in which the Court declared that the white primary was a violation of the Fifteenth Amendment. The Court reasoned that the political party was actually performing a state function and holding a primary election and therefore not acting as a private group.

WESTLAW Summary

Action by Lonnie E. Smith against S. E. Allwright, Election Judge, and James E. Liuzza, Associate Election Judge, Forty-Eighth Precinct of Harris County, Texas, for a declaratory judgment, and for damages due to the refusal of the defendants to permit the plaintiff to cast a ballot in a primary election for nomination of Democratic candidates for the United States Senate and House of Representatives, and Governor and other state officers. A judgment dismissing the petition was affirmed by the Circuit Court of Appeals. The Supreme Court granted certiorari and reversed.

Case Excerpts

Mr. Justice REED delivered the opinion of the Court.

This writ of certiorari brings here for review a claim for damages in the sum of $5,000 on the part of petitioner, a Negro citizen of the 48th precinct of Harris County, Texas, for the refusal of respondents, election and associate election judges respectively of that precinct, to give petitioner a ballot or to permit him to cast a ballot in the primary election of July 27, 1940, for the nomination of Democratic candidates for the United States Senate and House of Representatives, and Governor and other state officers. The refusal is alleged to have been solely because of the race and color of the proposed voter.

* * * *

The State of Texas by its Constitution and statutes provides that every person, if certain other requirements are met which are not here in issue, qualified by residence in the district or county "shall be deemed a qualified elector." Primary elections for United States Senators, Congressmen and state officers are provided for by * * * the statutes. Under these [statutes], the Democratic Party was required to hold the primary which was the occasion of the alleged wrong to petitioner. * * * These nominations are to be made by the qualified voters of the party.

The Democratic Party of Texas is held by the Supreme Court of that state to be a "voluntary association," protected by Section 27 of the Bill of Rights, Art[icle] 1, Constitution of Texas, from interference by the state except that:

"In the interest of fair methods and a fair expression by their members of their preferences in the selection of their nominees, the State may regulate such elections by proper laws." That court stated further:

"Since the right to organize and maintain a political party is one guaranteed by the Bill of Rights of this state, it necessarily follows that every privilege essential or reasonably appropriate to the exercise of that right is likewise guaranteed, including, of course, the privilege of determining the policies of the party and its membership. Without the privilege of determining the policy of a political association and its membership, the right to organize such an association would be a mere mockery. We think these rights, that is, the right to determine the membership of a political party and to determine its policies, of necessity are to be exercised by the State Convention of such party, and cannot, under any circumstances, be conferred upon a state or governmental agency."

The Democratic party on May 24, 1932, in a State Convention adopted the following resolution, which has not since been "amended, abrogated, annulled or avoided."

"Be it resolved that all white citizens of the State of Texas who are qualified to vote under the Constitution and laws of the State shall be eligible to membership in the Democratic party and, as such, entitled to participate in its deliberations." It was by virtue of this resolution that the respondents refused to permit the petitioner to vote.

Texas is free to conduct her elections and limit her electorate as she may deem wise, save only as her action may be affected by the prohibitions of the United States Constitution or in conflict with powers delegated to and exercised by the National Government. The Fourteenth Amendment forbids a state from making or enforcing any law which abridges the privileges or immunities of citizens of the United States and the Fifteenth Amendment specifically interdicts any denial or abridgement by a state of the right of citizens to vote on account of color. Respondents appeared in the District Court and the Circuit Court of Appeals and defended on the ground that the Democratic party of Texas is a voluntary organization with members banded together for the purpose of selecting individuals of the group representing the common political beliefs as candidates in the general election. As such a voluntary organization, it was claimed, the Democratic party is free to select its own membership and limit to whites participation in the party primary. Such action, the answer asserted, does not violate the Fourteenth, Fifteenth or Seventeenth Amendment as officers of government cannot be chosen at primaries and the Amendments are applicable only to general elections where governmental officers are actually elected. Primaries, it is said, are political party affairs, handled by party not governmental officers. * * *

* * * *

It may now be taken as a postulate that the right to vote in such a primary for the nomination of candidates without discrimination by the State, like the right to vote in a general election, is a right secured by the Constitution * * * By the terms of the Fifteenth Amendment that right may not be abridged by any state on account of race. Under our Constitution the great privilege of the ballot may not be denied a man by the State because of his color.

* * * *

We think that this statutory system for the selection of party nominees for inclusion on the general election ballot makes the party which is required to follow these legislative directions an agency of the state in so far as it determines the participants in a primary election. The party takes its character as a state agency from the duties imposed upon it by state statutes; the duties do not become matters of private law because they are performed by a political party. The plan of the Texas primary follows substantially that of Louisiana, with the exception that in Louisiana the state pays the cost of the primary while Texas assesses the cost against candidates. In numerous instances, the Texas statutes fix or limit the fees to be charged. Whether paid directly by the state or through state requirements, it is state action which compels. When primaries become a part of the machinery for choosing officials, state and national, as they have here, the same tests to determine the character of discrimination or abridgement should be applied to the primary as are applied to the general election. If the state requires a certain electoral procedure, prescribes a general election ballot made up of party nominees so chosen and limits the choice of the electorate in general elections for state offices, practically speaking, to those whose names appear on such a ballot, it endorses, adopts and enforces the discrimination against Negroes, practiced by a party entrusted by Texas law with the determination of the qualifications of participants in the primary. This is state action within the meaning of the Fifteenth Amendment.

The United States is a constitutional democracy. Its organic law grants to all citizens a right to participate in the choice of elected officials without restriction by any state because of race. This grant to the people of the opportunity for choice is not to be nullified by a state through casting its electoral process in a form which permits a private organization to practice racial discrimination in the election. Constitutional rights would be of little value if they could be thus indirectly denied.

The privilege of membership in a party may be no concern of a state. But when, as here, that privilege is also the essential qualification for voting in a primary to select nominees for a general election, the state makes the action of the party the action of the state. In reaching this conclusion we are not unmindful of the desirability of continuity of decision in constitutional questions. However, when convinced of former error, this Court has never felt constrained to follow precedent. In constitutional questions, where correction depends upon amendment and not upon legislative action this Court throughout its history has freely exercised its power to reexamine the basis of its constitutional decisions. This has long been accepted practice, and this practice has continued to this day. This is particularly true when the decision believed erroneous is the application of a constitutional principle rather than an interpretation of the Constitution to extract the principle itself. Here we are applying the well established principle of the Fifteenth Amendment, forbidding the abridgement by a state of a citizen's right to vote. * * *

Decision

Judgment reversed.

U.S. TERM LIMITS, INC., et al.
v.
Ray **THORNTON** et al.
514 U.S. 779, 115 S.Ct. 1842, 131 L.Ed.2d 881.
Argued Nov. 29, 1994.
Decided May 22, 1995.

Introduction

A case challenging an amendment to the Arkansas state constitution that established term limits for U.S. senators and representatives. The Court held that a state does not have the authority to establish term limits and that only an amendment to the U.S. Constitution could do so. The decision thus rendered invalid laws in approximately half of the states that had established term limits for U.S. congresspersons.

WESTLAW Summary

Action was brought challenging amendment to the Arkansas Constitution which precluded persons who had served certain number of terms in the United States Congress from having their names placed on the ballot for election to Congress. The Circuit Court found that the provision violated the United States Constitution. The Arkansas Supreme Court affirmed, 316 Ark. 251, 872 S.W.2d 349. On certiorari, the Supreme Court, Justice Stevens, held that: (1) states may not impose qualifications for offices of the United States representative or United States senator in addition to those set forth by the Constitution; (2) power to set additional qualifications was not reserved to the states by the Tenth Amendment; and (3) state provision is unconstitutional when it has likely effect of handicapping a class of candidates and has the sole purpose of creating additional qualifications indirectly.

Case Excerpts

Justice STEVENS delivered the opinion of the Court.
  * * * *

Today's cases present a challenge to an amendment to the Arkansas State Constitution that prohibits the name of an otherwise-eligible candidate for Congress from appearing on the general election ballot if that candidate has already served three terms in the House of Representatives or two terms in the Senate. The Arkansas Supreme Court held that the amendment violates the Federal Constitution. We agree with that holding. * * *

* * * *

Twenty-six years ago, in *Powell v. McCormack*, we reviewed the history and text of the Qualifications Clauses in a case involving an attempted exclusion of a duly elected Member of Congress. The principal issue was whether the power granted to each House in Art. I, s 5, to judge the "Qualifications of its own Members" includes the power to impose qualifications other than those set forth in the text of the Constitution. In an opinion by Chief Justice Warren for eight Members of the Court, we held that it does not. * * *

* * * *

* * * [O]ur historical analysis in *Powell* was both detailed and persuasive. We thus conclude now, as we did in *Powell*, that history shows that, with respect to Congress, the Framers intended the Constitution to establish fixed qualifications.

In *Powell*, of course, we did not rely solely on an analysis of the historical evidence, but instead complemented that analysis with "an examination of the basic principles of our democratic system." We noted that allowing Congress to impose additional qualifications would violate that "fundamental principle of our representative democracy ... 'that the people should choose whom they please to govern them.' "

* * * *

Our opinion made clear that this broad principle incorporated at least two fundamental ideas. First, we emphasized the egalitarian concept that the opportunity to be elected was open to all.* * *

Second, we recognized the critical postulate that sovereignty is vested in the people, and that sovereignty confers on the people the right to choose freely their representatives to the National Government. * * *

Powell thus establishes two important propositions: first, that the "relevant historical materials" compel the conclusion that, at least with respect to qualifications imposed by Congress, the Framers intended the qualifications listed in the Constitution to be exclusive; and second, that that conclusion is equally compelled by an understanding of the "fundamental principle of our representative democracy ... 'that the people should choose whom they please to govern them.' "

* * * *

Our reaffirmation of *Powell,* does not necessarily resolve the specific questions presented in these cases. For petitioners argue that whatever the constitutionality of additional qualifications for membership imposed by Congress, the historical and textual materials discussed in *Powell* do not support the conclusion that the Constitution prohibits additional qualifications imposed by States. In the absence of such a constitutional prohibition, petitioners argue, the Tenth Amendment and the principle of reserved powers require that States be allowed to add such qualifications.

* * * *

Contrary to petitioners' assertions, the power to add qualifications is not part of the original powers of sovereignty that the Tenth Amendment reserved to the States. Petitioners' Tenth Amendment argument misconceives the nature of the right at issue because that Amendment could only "reserve" that which existed before. * * *

* * * *

With respect to setting qualifications for service in Congress, no such right existed before the Constitution was ratified. The contrary argument overlooks the revolutionary character of the government that the Framers conceived. Prior to the adoption of the Constitution, the States had joined together under the Articles of Confederation. In that system, "the States retained most of their sovereignty, like independent nations bound together only by treaties." After the Constitutional Convention convened, the Framers were presented with, and eventually adopted a variation of, "a plan not merely to amend the Articles of Confederation but to create an entirely new National Government with a National Executive, National Judiciary, and a National Legislature." In adopting

that plan, the Framers envisioned a uniform national system, rejecting the notion that the Nation was a collection of States, and instead creating a direct link between the National Government and the people of the United States. In that National Government, representatives owe primary allegiance not to the people of a State, but to the people of the Nation. * * *
* * * *

In short, as the Framers recognized, electing representatives to the National Legislature was a new right, arising from the Constitution itself. The Tenth Amendment thus provides no basis for concluding that the States possess reserved power to add qualifications to those that are fixed in the Constitution. Instead, any state power to set the qualifications for membership in Congress must derive not from the reserved powers of state sovereignty, but rather from the delegated powers of national sovereignty. In the absence of any constitutional delegation to the States of power to add qualifications to those enumerated in the Constitution, such a power does not exist.
* * * *

Our conclusion that States lack the power to impose qualifications vindicates the same "fundamental principle of our representative democracy" that we recognized in *Powell*, namely that "the people should choose whom they please to govern them."

As we noted earlier, the *Powell* Court recognized that an egalitarian ideal—that election to the National Legislature should be open to all people of merit—provided a critical foundation for the Constitutional structure. This egalitarian theme echoes throughout the constitutional debates. In *The Federalist* No. 57, for example, Madison wrote: "Who are to be the objects of popular choice? Every citizen whose merit may recommend him to the esteem and confidence of his country. No qualification of wealth, of birth, of religious faith, or of civil profession is permitted to fetter the judgment or disappoint the inclination of the people."
* * * *

Similarly, we believe that state-imposed qualifications, as much as congressionally imposed qualifications, would undermine the second critical idea recognized in *Powell:* that an aspect of sovereignty is the right of the people to vote for whom they wish. Again, the source of the qualification is of little moment in assessing the qualification's restrictive impact.

Finally, state-imposed restrictions, unlike the congressionally imposed restrictions at issue in *Powell,* violate a third idea central to this basic principle: that the right to choose representatives belongs not to the States, but to the people. * * *
* * * *

Consistent with these views, the constitutional structure provides for a uniform salary to be paid from the national treasury, allows the States but a limited role in federal elections, and maintains strict checks on state interference with the federal election process. The Constitution also provides that the qualifications of the representatives of each State will be judged by the representatives of the entire Nation. The Constitution thus creates a uniform national body representing the interests of a single people.

Permitting individual States to formulate diverse qualifications for their representatives would result in a patchwork of state qualifications, undermining the uniformity and the national character that the Framers envisioned and sought to ensure. Such a patchwork would also sever the direct link that the Framers found so critical between the National Government and the people of the United States.
* * * *

In sum, the available historical and textual evidence, read in light of the basic principles of democracy underlying the Constitution and recognized by this Court in *Powell,* reveal the Framers' intent that neither Congress nor the States should possess the power to supplement the exclusive qualifications set forth in the text of the Constitution.
* * * *

The merits of term limits, or "rotation," have been the subject of debate since the formation of our Constitution, when the Framers unanimously rejected a proposal to add such limits to the Constitution. The cogent arguments on both sides of the question that were articulated during the process of ratification largely retain their force today. Over half the States have adopted measures that impose such limits on some offices either directly or indirectly, and the Nation as a whole, notably by constitutional amendment, has imposed a limit on the number of terms that the President may serve. Term limits, like any other qualification for office, unquestionably restrict the ability of voters to vote for whom they wish. On the other hand, such limits may provide for the infusion of fresh ideas and new perspectives, and may decrease the likelihood that representatives will lose touch with their constituents. It is not our province to resolve this longstanding debate.

We are, however, firmly convinced that allowing the several States to adopt term limits for congressional service would effect a fundamental change in the constitutional framework. Any such change must come not by legislation adopted either by Congress or by an individual State, but rather—as have other important changes in the electoral process—through the Amendment procedures set forth in Article V. The Framers decided that the qualifications for service in the Congress of the United States be fixed in the Constitution and be uniform throughout the Nation. That decision reflects the Framers' understanding that Members of Congress are chosen by separate constituencies, but that they become, when elected, servants of the people of the United States. They are not merely delegates appointed by separate, sovereign States; they occupy offices that are integral and essential components of a single National Government. In the absence of a properly passed constitutional amendment, allowing individual States to craft their own qualifications for Congress would thus erode the structure envisioned by the Framers, a structure that was designed, in the words of the Preamble to our Constitution, to form a "more perfect Union."

Decision

The judgment is affirmed.

International Union, **UNITED AUTOMOBILE,** Aerospace and
Agricultural Implement **WORKERS** of America, UAW, et al.
v.
JOHNSON CONTROLS, INC.
111 S.Ct. 1196, 113 L.Ed.2d 158.
Argued Oct. 10, 1990.
Decided March 20, 1991.

Introduction

A Sex discrimination case in which the Supreme Court held that a company's fetal protection policy that excluded women from possibly hazardous employment conditions constituted sex discrimination under Title VII of the 1964 Civil Rights Act.

WESTLAW Summary

Class action was brought challenging employer's policy barring all women, except those whose infertility was medically documented, from jobs involving actual or potential lead exposure exceeding Occupational Safety and Health Administration (OSHA) standard. The United States District Court for the Eastern District of Wisconsin granted summary judgment for employer. On appeal, the Court of Appeals for the Seventh Circuit affirmed, and certiorari was granted. The Supreme Court, Justice Blackmun, held that: (1) employer's policy was facially discriminatory, and (2) employer did not establish that sex was a bona fide occupational qualification (BFOQ).

Case Excerpts

Justice BLACKMUN delivered the opinion of the Court.

In this case we are concerned with an employer's gender-based fetal-protection policy. May an employer exclude a fertile female employee from certain jobs because of its concern for the health of the fetus the woman might conceive?

Respondent Johnson Controls, Inc., manufactures batteries. In the manufacturing process, the element lead is a primary ingredient. Occupational exposure to lead entails health risks, including the risk of harm to any fetus carried by a female employee.

Before the Civil Rights Act of 1964 became law, Johnson Controls did not employ any woman in a battery-manufacturing job. In June 1977, however, it announced its first official policy concerning its employment of women in lead-exposure work * * *
* * * *

Five years later, in 1982, Johnson Controls shifted from a policy of warning to a policy of exclusion. * * * "... [I]t is [Johnson Controls'] policy that women who are pregnant or who are capable of bearing children will not be placed into jobs involving lead exposure or which could expose them to lead through the exercise of job bidding, bumping, transfer or promotion rights." * * *

In April 1984, petitioners filed in the United States District Court for the Eastern District of Wisconsin a class action challenging Johnson Controls' fetal-protection policy as sex discrimination that violated Title VII of the Civil Rights Act of 1964, as amended. * * *
* * * *

The bias in Johnson Controls' policy is obvious. Fertile men, but not fertile women, are given a choice as to whether they wish to risk their reproductive health for a particular job. Section 703(a) of the Civil Rights Act of 1964 prohibits sex-based classifications in terms and conditions of employment, in hiring and discharging decisions, and in other employment decisions that adversely affect an employee's status. Respondent's fetal-protection policy explicitly discriminates against women on the basis of their sex. The policy excludes women with childbearing capacity from lead-exposed jobs and so creates a facial classification based on gender. * * *

* * * *

* * * Johnson Controls' policy classifies on the basis of gender and childbearing capacity, rather than fertility alone. Respondent does not seek to protect the unconceived children of all its employees. Despite evidence in the record about the debilitating effect of lead exposure on the male reproductive system, Johnson Controls is concerned only with the harms that may befall the unborn offspring of its female employees. * * * Johnson Controls' policy is facially discriminatory because it requires only a female employee to produce proof that she is not capable of reproducing.

* * * *

Under [Section] 703(e)(1) of Title VII, an employer may discriminate on the basis of "religion, sex, or national origin in those certain instances where religion, sex, or national origin is a bona fide occupational qualification [BFOQ] reasonably necessary to the normal operation of that particular business or enterprise." * * *

* * * *

Johnson Controls argues that its fetal-protection policy falls within the so-called safety exception to the BFOQ. Our cases have stressed that discrimination on the basis of sex because of safety concerns is allowed only in narrow circumstances. * * *

* * * *

Our case law * * * makes clear that the safety exception is limited to instances in which sex or pregnancy actually interferes with the employee's ability to perform the job. This approach is consistent with the language of the BFOQ provision itself, for it suggests that permissible distinctions based on sex must relate to ability to perform the duties of the job. Johnson Controls suggests, however, that we expand the exception to allow fetal-protection policies that mandate particular standards for pregnant or fertile women. We decline to do so. Such an expansion contradicts not only the language of the BFOQ and the narrowness of its exception but the plain language and history of the Pregnancy Discrimination Act.

The [Pregnancy Discrimination Act's] amendment to Title VII contains a BFOQ standard of its own: unless pregnant employees differ from others "in their ability or inability to work," they must be "treated the same" as other employees "for all employment-related purposes." This language clearly sets forth Congress' remedy for discrimination on the basis of pregnancy and potential pregnancy. Women who are either pregnant or potentially pregnant must be treated like others "similar in their ability ... to work." In other words, women as capable of doing their jobs as their male counterparts may not be forced to choose between having a child and having a job.

* * * *

We have no difficulty concluding that Johnson Controls cannot establish a BFOQ. Fertile women, as far as appears in the record, participate in the manufacture of batteries as efficiently as anyone else. Johnson Controls' professed moral and ethical concerns about the welfare of the next generation do not suffice to establish a BFOQ of female sterility. Decisions about the welfare of future children must be left to the parents who conceive, bear, support, and raise them rather than to the employers who hire those parents. Congress has mandated this choice through Title VII, as amended by the Pregnancy Discrimination Act. Johnson Controls has attempted to exclude women because of their reproductive capacity. Title VII and the PDA simply do not allow a woman's dismissal because of her failure to submit to sterilization.

Nor can concerns about the welfare of the next generation be considered a part of the "essence" of Johnson Controls' business. * * *

* * * *

Our holding today that Title VII, as so amended, forbids sex-specific fetal-protection policies is neither remarkable nor unprecedented. Concern for a woman's existing or potential offspring historically has been the excuse for denying women equal employment opportunities. Congress in the PDA prohibited discrimination on the basis of a woman's ability to become pregnant. We do no more than hold that the Pregnancy Discrimination Act means what it says.

It is no more appropriate for the courts than it is for individual employers to decide whether a woman's reproductive role is more important to herself and her family than her economic role. Congress has left this choice to the woman as hers to make.

Decision

The judgment of the Court of Appeals is reversed and the case is remanded for further proceedings consistent with this opinion.

UNITED STATES
v.
HARRISS, et al.
347 U.S. 612, 74 S.Ct. 80898, L.Ed. 989.
Argued Oct. 19, 1953.
Decided June 7, 1954.

Introduction

A First Amendment case challenging the constitutional validity of the Federal Regulation of Lobbying Act. The Supreme Court held that the act did not violate the appellants' rights under the First Amendment.

WESTLAW Summary

Defendants were charged by information with violation of the Federal Regulation of Lobbying Act. The United States District Court for the District of Columbia dismissed the information on ground that the Act is unconstitutional, and the government's appeal was taken directly to Supreme Court, under the Criminal Appeals Act. The Supreme Court, Mr. Chief Justice Warren, held that the Act meets the constitutional requirement of definiteness, and that the sections thereof, under which the information was laid, do not violate constitutional guarantees of freedom to speak, publish and petition the government.

Case Excerpts

Mr. Chief Justice WARREN delivered the opinion of the Court.

The appellees were charged by information with violation of the Federal Regulation of Lobbying Act. * * * [T]he District Court dismissed the information on the ground that the Act is unconstitutional. The case is here on direct appeal under the Criminal Appeals Act.

* * * *

* * * Our review under the Criminal Appeals Act is limited to a decision on the alleged "invalidity" of the statute on which the information is based. In making this decision, we judge the statute on its face. The "invalidity" of the Lobbying Act is asserted on three grounds: (1) that [Sections] 305, 307, and 308 are too vague and indefinite to meet the requirements of due process; (2) that [Sections] 305 and 308 violate the First Amendment guarantees of freedom of speech, freedom of the press, and the right to petition the Government; (3) that the penalty provision of [Section] 310(b) violates the right of the people under the First Amendment to petition the Government.

The constitutional requirement of definiteness is violated by a criminal statute that fails to give a person of ordinary intelligence fair notice that his contemplated conduct is forbidden by the statute. The underlying principle is that no man shall be held criminally responsible for conduct which he could not reasonably understand to be proscribed.

On the other hand, if the general class of offenses to which the statute is directed is plainly within its terms, the statute will not be struck down as vague even though marginal cases could be put where doubts might arise. And if this general class of offenses can be made constitutionally definite by a reasonable construction of the statute, this Court is under a duty to give the statute that construction. * * *

The same course is appropriate here. The key section of the Lobbying Act is [Section] 307, entitled "Persons to Whom Applicable." Section 307 provides: "The provisions of this title shall apply to any person (except a political committee as defined in the Federal Corrupt Practices Act, and duly organized State or local committees of a political party), who by himself, or through any agent or employee or other persons in any manner whatsoever, directly or indirectly, solicits, collects, or receives money or any other thing of value to be used principally to aid, or the principal purpose of which person is to aid, in the accomplishment of any of the following purposes: '(a) The passage or defeat of any legislation by the Congress of the United States.' '(b) To influence, directly or indirectly, the passage or defeat of any legislation by the Congress of the United States.' This section modifies the substantive provisions of the Act, including [Section] 305 and [Section] 308. In other words, unless a 'person' falls within the category established by [Section] 307, the disclosure requirements of [Section] 305 and [Section] 308 are inapplicable. Thus coverage under the Act is limited to those persons (except for the specified political committees) who solicit, collect, or receive contributions of money or other thing of value, and then only if the principal purpose of either the persons or the contributions is to aid in the accomplishment of the aims set forth in [Section] 307(a) and (b)." In any event, the solicitation, collection, or receipt of money or other thing of value is a prerequisite to coverage under the Act.

* * * *

We now turn to the alleged vagueness of the purposes set forth in [Section] 307(a) and (b). * * * [W]e believe this language should be construed to refer only to "lobbying in its commonly accepted sense"—to direct communication with members of Congress on pending or proposed federal legislation. The legislative history of the Act makes clear that, at the very least, Congress sought disclosure of such direct pressures, exerted by the lobbyists themselves or through their hirelings or through an artificially stimulated letter campaign. It is likewise clear that Congress would have intended the Act to operate on this narrower basis, even if a broader application to organizations seeking to propagandize the general public were not permissible.

There remains for our consideration the meaning of "the principal purpose" and "to be used principally to aid." The legislative history of the Act indicates that the term "principal" was adopted merely to exclude from the scope of [Section] 307 those contributions and persons having only an "incidental" purpose of influencing legislation. Conversely, the "principal purpose" requirement does not exclude a contribution which in substantial part is to be used to influence legislation through direct communication with Congress or a person whose activities in substantial part are directed to influencing legislation through direct communication with Congress. If it were otherwise—if an organization, for example, were exempted because lobbying was only one of its main activities—the Act would in large measure be reduced to a mere exhortation against abuse of the legislative process. In construing the Act narrowly to avoid constitutional doubts, we must also avoid a construction that would seriously impair the effectiveness of the Act in coping with the problem it was designed to alleviate.

To summarize, therefore, there are three prerequisites to coverage under [Section] 307: (1) the "person" must have solicited, collected, or received contributions; (2) one of the main purposes of such "person," or one of the main purposes of such contributions, must have been to influence the passage or defeat of legislation by Congress; (3) the intended method of accomplishing this purpose must have been through direct communication with members of Congress. And since [Section] 307 modifies the substantive provisions of the Act, our construction of [Section] 307 will of necessity also narrow the scope of [Section] 305 and [Section] 308, the substantive provisions underlying the information in this case. Thus [Section] 305 is limited to those persons who are covered by [Section] 307; and when so covered, they must report all contributions and expenditures having the purpose of attempting to influence legislation through direct communication with Congress. Similarly, [Section] 308 is limited to those persons (with the stated exceptions) who are covered by [Section] 307 and who, in addition, engage themselves for pay or for any other valuable consideration for the purpose of attempting to influence legislation through direct communication with Congress. Construed in this way, the Lobbying Act meets the constitutional requirement of definiteness.

Thus construed, [Sections] 305 and 308 also do not violate the freedoms guaranteed by the First Amendment—freedom to speak, publish, and petition the Government.

* * * *

* * * [Congress] has * * * provided for a modicum of information from those who for hire attempt to influence legislation or who collect or spend funds for that purpose. It wants only to know who is being hired, who is putting up the money, and how much. * * *

Under these circumstances, we believe that Congress, at least within the bounds of the Act as we have construed it, is not constitutionally forbidden to require the disclosure of lobbying activities. To do so would be to deny Congress in large measure the power of self-protection. And here Congress has used that power in a manner restricted to its appropriate end. We conclude that [Sections] 305 and 308, as applied to persons defined in [Section] 307, do not offend the First Amendment.

Decision

Reversed.

UNITED STATES
v.
Richard M. **NIXON**, et al.
418 U.S. 683, 94 S.Ct. 3090, 41 L.Ed.2d 1039.
Argued July 8, 1974.
Decided July 24, 1974.

Introduction

A presidential executive privilege case in which the Court ruled that President Nixon had to hand over secret tapes containing his Oval Office conversations while in the White House. The Court ruled that executive privilege could not be used to prevent evidence from being heard in criminal proceedings.

WESTLAW Summary

Prosecution of former government officials and presidential campaign officials for conspiracy to defraud the United States and to obstruct justice, and for other offenses, wherein the special prosecutor caused a third-party subpoena duces tecum to be issued directing the President to produce tape recordings and documents relating to conversations with aides and advisors. The United States District Court for the District of Columbia denied the President's motion to quash subpoena and an appeal was taken. Certiorari before judgment was granted to bring the matter before the Supreme Court before disposition by the Court of Appeals. The Supreme Court held that the dispute was justiciable; that the District Court was not shown to have erred in determining that the special prosecutor's showing of relevancy, admissibility, and specificity was sufficient to warrant the issuance of the order; and that the President's generalized interest in confidentiality, unsupported by a claim of need to protect military, diplomatic, or sensitive national security secrets could not prevail against the special prosecutor's demonstrated, specific need for the tape recordings and documents.

Case Excerpts

Mr. Chief Justice BURGER delivered the opinion of the Court.

This litigation presents for review the denial of a motion, filed in the District Court on behalf of the President of the United States * * * to quash a third-party subpoena duces tecum issued by the United States District Court for the District of Columbia. The subpoena directed the President to produce certain tape recordings and documents relating to his conversations with aides and advisers. The court rejected the President's claims of absolute executive privilege, of lack of jurisdiction, and of failure to satisfy the requirements of Rule 17(c). The President appealed to the Court of Appeals. We granted both the United States' petition for certiorari before judgment and also the President's cross-petition for certiorari before judgment because of the public importance of the issues presented and the need for their prompt resolution

On March 1, 1974, a grand jury of the United States District Court for the District of Columbia returned an indictment charging seven named individuals with various offenses, including conspiracy to defraud the United States and to obstruct justice. Although he was not designated as such in the indictment, the grand jury named the President, among others, as an unindicted coconspirator. On April 18, 1974, upon motion of the Special Prosecutor, a subpoena duces tecum was issued pursuant to Rule 17(c) to the President by the United States District Court and made returnable on May 2, 1974. This subpoena required the production, in advance of the September 9 trial date, of certain tapes, memoranda, papers, transcripts or other writings relating to certain precisely identified meetings between the President and others. * * * On April 30, the President publicly released edited transcripts of 43 conversations; portions of 20 conversations subject to subpoena in the present case were included. On May 1, 1974, the President's counsel, filed a "special appearance" and a motion to quash the subpoena under Rule 17(c). This motion was accompanied by a formal claim of privilege. At a subsequent hearing, further motions to expunge the grand jury's action naming the President as an unindicted coconspirator and for protective orders against the disclosure of that information were filed or raised orally by counsel for the President.

On May 20, 1974, the District Court denied the motion to quash and the motions to expunge and for protective orders. It further ordered "the President or any subordinate officer, official, or employee with custody or control of the documents or objects subpoenaed," to deliver to the District Court, on or before May 31, 1974, the originals of all subpoenaed items, as well as an index and analysis of those items, together with tape copies of those portions of the subpoenaed recordings for which transcripts had been released to the public by the President on April 30. The District Court rejected jurisdictional challenges based on a contention that the dispute was nonjusticiable because it was between the Special Prosecutor and the Chief Executive and hence "intra-executive" in character; it also rejected the contention that the Judiciary was without authority to review an assertion of executive privilege by the President. * * *

The District Court held that the judiciary, not the President, was the final arbiter of a claim of executive privilege. The court concluded that under the circumstances of this case the presumptive privilege was overcome by the Special Prosecutor's prima facie "demonstration of need sufficiently compelling to warrant judicial examination in chambers . . . ." * * *

* * * *

In the performance of assigned constitutional duties each branch of the Government must initially interpret the Constitution, and the interpretation of its powers by any branch is due great respect from the others. The President's counsel, as we have noted, reads the Constitution as providing an absolute privilege of confidentiality for all Presidential communications. Many decisions of this Court, however, have unequivocally reaffirmed the holding of *Marbury v. Madison* that "(i)t is emphatically the province and duty of the judicial department to say what the law is."

No holding of the Court has defined the scope of judicial power specifically relating to the enforcement of a subpoena for confidential Presidential communications for use in a criminal prosecution, but other exercises of power by the Executive Branch and the Legislative Branch have been found invalid as in conflict with the Constitution. * * * Since this Court has consistently exercised the power to construe and delineate claims arising under express powers, it must follow that the Court has authority to interpret claims with respect to powers alleged to derive from enumerated powers.

* * * *

Notwithstanding the deference each branch must accord the others, the "judicial Power of the United States" vested in the federal courts by Art[icle] III, [Section] 1, of the Constitution can no more be shared with the Executive Branch than the Chief Executive, for example, can share with the Judiciary the veto power, or the Congress share with the Judiciary the power to override a Presidential veto. Any other conclusion would be contrary to the basic concept of separation of powers and the checks and balances that flow from the scheme of a tripartite government. We therefore reaffirm that it is the province and duty of this Court "to say what the law is" with respect to the claim of privilege presented in this case.

In support of his claim of absolute privilege, the President's counsel urges two grounds, one of which is common to all governments and one of which is peculiar to our system of separation of powers. The first ground is the valid need for protection of communications between high Government officials and those who advise and assist them in the performance of their manifold duties; the importance of this confidentiality is too plain to require further discussion. Human experience teaches that those who expect public dissemination of their remarks may well temper candor with a concern for appearances and for their own interests to the detriment of the decisionmaking process. Whatever the nature of the privilege of confidentiality of Presidential communications in the exercise of Art[icle] II powers, the privilege can be said to derive from the supremacy of each branch within its own assigned area of constitutional duties. Certain powers and privileges flow from the nature of enumerated powers; the protection of the confidentiality of Presidential communications has similar constitutional underpinnings.

The second ground asserted by the President's counsel in support of the claim of absolute privilege rests on the doctrine of separation of powers. Here it is argued that the independence of the Executive Branch within its own sphere insulates a President from a judicial subpoena in an ongoing criminal prosecution, and thereby protects confidential Presidential communications.

However, neither the doctrine of separation of powers, nor the need for confidentiality of high-level communications, without more, can sustain an absolute, unqualified Presidential privilege of immunity from judicial process under all circumstances. The President's need for complete candor and objectivity from advisers calls for great deference from the courts. However, when the privilege depends solely on the broad, undifferentiated claim of public interest in the confidentiality of such conversations, a confrontation with other values arises. Absent a claim of need to protect military, diplomatic, or sensitive national security secrets, we find it difficult to accept the argument that even the very important interest in confidentiality of Presidential communications is significantly diminished by production of such material for in camera inspection with all the protection that a district court will be obliged to provide.

The impediment that an absolute, unqualified privilege would place in the way of the primary constitutional duty of the Judicial Branch to do justice in criminal prosecutions would plainly conflict with the function of the courts under Art[icle] III. In designing the structure of our Government and dividing and allocating the sovereign power among three co-equal branches, the Framers of the Constitution sought to provide a comprehensive system, but the separate powers were not intended to operate with absolute independence.

* * * *

Since we conclude that the legitimate needs of the judicial process may outweigh Presidential privilege, it is necessary to resolve those competing interests in a manner that preserves the essential functions of each branch. The right and indeed the duty to resolve that question does not free the Judiciary from according high respect to the representations made on behalf of the President.

The expectation of a President to the confidentiality of his conversations and correspondence, like the claim of confidentiality of judicial deliberations, for example, has all the values to which we accord deference for the privacy of all citizens and, added to those values, is the necessity for protection of the public interest in candid, objective, and even blunt or harsh opinions in Presidential decisionmaking. A President and those who assist him must be free to explore alternatives in the process of shaping policies and making decisions and to do so in a way many would be unwilling to express except privately. These are the considerations justifying a presumptive privilege for Presidential communications. The privilege is fundamental to the operation of Government and inextricably rooted in the separation of powers under the Constitution. * * *

But this presumptive privilege must be considered in light of our historic commitment to the rule of law. * * * The very integrity of the judicial system and public confidence in the system depend on full disclosure of all the facts, within the framework of the rules of evidence. To ensure that justice is done, it is imperative to the function of courts that compulsory process be available for the production of evidence needed either by the prosecution or by the defense.

* * * *

* * * Nowhere in the Constitution, as we have noted earlier, is there any explicit reference to a privilege of confidentiality, yet to the extent this interest relates to the effective discharge of a President's powers, it is constitutionally based.

* * * *

We conclude that when the ground for asserting privilege as to subpoenaed materials sought for use in a criminal trial is based only on the generalized interest in confidentiality, it cannot prevail over the fundamental demands of due process of law in the fair administration of criminal justice. The generalized assertion of privilege must yield to the demonstrated, specific need for evidence in a pending criminal trial.

* * * Since this matter came before the Court during the pendency of a criminal prosecution, and on representations that time is of the essence, the mandate shall issue forthwith.

Decision

Affirmed.

UNITED STATES CIVIL SERVICE COMMISSION et al.
v.
NATIONAL ASSOCIATION OF LETTER CARRIERS AFL-CIO, et al.
413 U.S. 548, 93 S.Ct. 2880, 37 L.Ed.2d 796.
Argued March 26, 1973.
Decided June 25, 1973.

Introduction

A First Amendment/constitutional rights case in which the Supreme Court upheld the validity of the Hatch Act's prohibitions against the participation of federal employees in political campaigns.

WESTLAW Summary

Declaratory judgment action to contest validity of Hatch Act prohibition against federal employees taking an active part in political management or in political campaigns. A three-judge panel of the United States District Court for the District of Columbia held such statutory provision unconstitutional as vague and overbroad, and the government appealed. The United States Supreme Court, Mr. Justice White, held that Hatch Act prohibitions were neither unconstitutionally vague nor fatally overbroad.

Case Excerpts

Mr. Justice WHITE delivered the opinion of the Court.

On December 11, 1972, we noted probable jurisdiction of this appeal, based on a jurisdictional statement presenting the single question whether the prohibition in [Section] 9(a) of the Hatch Act, * * * against federal employees taking "an active part in political management or in political campaigns," is unconstitutional on its face. Section 7324(a) provides: "An employee in an Executive agency or an individual employed by the government of the District of Columbia may not—"(1) use his official authority or influence for the purpose of interfering with or affecting the result of an election;" or "(2) take an active part in political management or in political campaigns." For the purpose of this subsection, the phrase "an active part in political management or in political campaigns" means those acts of political management or political campaigning which were prohibited on the part of employees in the competitive service before July 19, 1940, by determinations of the Civil Service Commission under the rules prescribed by the President."

The case began when the National Association of Letter Carriers, six individual federal employees and certain local Democratic and Republican political committees filed a complaint, asserting on behalf of themselves and all federal employees that 5 U.S.C. [Section] 7324(a)(2) was unconstitutional on its face and seeking an injunction against its enforcement.

Each of the plaintiffs alleged that the Civil Service Commission was enforcing, or threatening to enforce, the Hatch Act's prohibition against active participation in political management or political campaigns with respect to certain defined activity in which that plaintiff desired to engage. * * *

* * * The District Court then ruled that [Section] 7234(a)(2) was unconstitutional on its face and enjoined its enforcement. The court recognized the "well-established governmental interest in restricting political activities by federal employees which (had been) asserted long before enactment of the Hatch Act," as well as the fact that the "appropriateness of this governmental objective was recognized by the Supreme Court of the United States when it endorsed the objectives of the Hatch Act [in *United Public Workers v. Mitchell*]." The District Court ruled, however, that *United Public Workers v. Mitchell* left open the constitutionality of the statutory definition of "political activity" and proceeded to hold that definition to be both vague and overbroad, and therefore unconstitutional and unenforceable against the plaintiffs in any respect.

The District Court also added that even if the Supreme Court in *Mitchell* could be said to have upheld the definitional section in its entirety, later decisions had so eroded the holding that it could no longer be considered binding on the District Court.

* * * *

We unhesitatingly reaffirm the *Mitchell* holding that Congress had, and has, the power to prevent Mr. Poole and others like him from holding a party office, working at the polls, and acting as party paymaster for other party workers. An Act of Congress going no farther would in our view unquestionably be valid. So would it be if, in plain and understandable language, the statute forbade activities such as organizing a political party or club; actively participating in fund-raising activities for a partisan candidate or political party; becoming a partisan candidate for, or campaigning for, an elective public office; actively managing the campaign of a partisan candidate for public office; initiating or circulating a partisan nominating petition or soliciting votes for a partisan candidate for public office; or serving as a delegate, alternate or proxy to a political party convention. Our judgment is that neither the First Amendment nor any other provision of the Constitution invalidates a law barring this kind of partisan political conduct by federal employees.

* * * *

Until now, the judgment of Congress, the Executive, and the country appears to have been that partisan political activities by federal employees must be limited if the Government is to operate effectively and fairly, elections are to play their proper part in representative government, and employees themselves are to be sufficiently free from improper influences. The restrictions so far imposed on federal employees are not aimed at particular parties, groups, or points of view, but apply equally to all partisan activities of the type described. They discriminate against no racial, ethnic, or religious minorities. Nor do they seek to control political opinions or beliefs, or to interfere with or influence anyone's vote at the polls.

* * * Although Congress is free to strike a different balance than it has, if it so chooses, we think the balance it has so far struck is sustainable by the obviously important interests sought to be served by the limitations on partisan political activities now contained in the Hatch Act.

It seems fundamental in the first place that employees in the Executive Branch of the Government, or those working for any of its agencies, should administer the law in accordance with the will of Congress, rather than in accordance with their own or the will of a political party. They are expected to enforce the law and execute the programs of the Government without bias or favoritism for or against any political party or group or the members thereof. A major thesis of the Hatch Act is that to serve this great end of Government—the impartial execution of the laws—it is essential that federal employees, for example, not take formal positions in political parties, not undertake to play substantial roles in partisan political campaigns, and not run for office on partisan political tickets. Forbidding activities like these will reduce the hazards to fair and effective government.

* * * *

A related concern, and this remains as important as any other, was to further serve the goal that employment and advancement in the Government service not depend on political performance, and at the same time to make sure that Government employees would be free from pressure and from express or tacit invitation to vote in a certain way or perform political chores in order to curry favor with their superiors rather than to act out their own beliefs. It may be urged that prohibitions against coercion are sufficient protection; but for many years the joint judgment of the Executive and Congress has been that to protect the rights of federal employees with respect to their jobs and their political acts and beliefs it is not enough merely to forbid one employee to attempt to influence or coerce another. * * *

Neither the right to associate nor the right to participate in political activities is absolute in any event. Nor are the management, financing, and conduct of political campaigns wholly free from governmental regulation. We agree with the basic holding of *Mitchell* that plainly identifiable acts of political management and political campaigning on the part of federal employees may constitutionally be prohibited. Until now this has been the judgment of the lower federal courts, and we do not understand the District Court in this case to have questioned the constitutionality of a law that was specifically limited to prohibiting the conduct in which Mr. Poole in the *Mitchell* case admittedly engaged.

But however constitutional the proscription of identifiable partisan conduct in understandable language may be, the District Court's judgment was that [Section] 7324(a)(2) was both unconstitutionally vague and fatally overbroad. Appellees make the same contentions here, but we cannot agree that the section is unconstitutional on its face for either reason.

* * * *

The Act permits the individual employee to "express his opinion on political subjects and candidates"; and the corresponding [Civil Service Commission] regulation, 5 CFR [Section] 733.111(a)(2), privileges the employee to "(e)xpress his opinion as an individual privately and publicly on political subjects and candidates. * * * Arguably, there are problems in meshing [Section] 733.111(a)(2) with [Sections] 733.122(a)(10) ["endorsing or opposing a partisan candidate for public office or political party office in a political advertisement, a broadcast, campaign literature, or similar material"] and (12) ["addressing a convention, caucus, rally, or similar gathering of a political party in support of or in opposition to a partisan candidate for public office or political party office,"] but we think the latter prohibitions sufficiently clearly carve out the prohibited political conduct from the expressive activity permitted by the prior section to survive any attack on the ground of vagueness or in the name of any of those policies that doctrine may be deemed to further.

* * * *

Neither do we discern anything fatally overbroad about the statute when it is considered in connection with the Commission's construction of its terms represented by the 1970 regulations we now have before us. The major difficulties in this respect again relate to the prohibition in [Sections] 733.122(a) (10) and (12) * * *. But these restrictions are clearly stated, they are political acts normally performed only in the context of partisan campaigns by one taking an active role in them, and they are sustainable for the same reasons that the other acts of political campaigning are constitutionally proscribable. They do not, therefore, render the remainder of the statute vulnerable by reason of over-breadth.

Even if the provisions forbidding partisan campaign endorsements and speechmaking were to be considered in some respects unconstitutionally overbroad, we would not invalidate the entire statute as the District Court did. The remainder of the statute, as we have said, covers a whole range of easily identifiable and constitutionally proscribable partisan conduct on the part of federal employees, and the extent to which pure expression is impermissibly threatened, if at all, by [Sections] 733.122(a)(10) and (12), does not in our view make the statute substantially overbroad and so invalid on its face.

Decision

For the foregoing reasons, the judgment of the District Court is reversed.

UNITED STEELWORKERS OF AMERICA, AFL-CIO-CLC
v.
Brian F. **WEBER** et al.
443 U.S. 193, 99 S.Ct. 2721, 61 L.Ed.2d 480.
Argued March 28, 1979.
Decided June 27, 1979.

Introduction

A civil rights/reverse discrimination case in which a union apprenticeship program that used a racial quota was deemed legal even if it violated the words of the Civil Rights Act of 1964 because it did not violate the spirit. Essentially, any form of reverse discrimination—even explicit quotas—is permissible provided that it is the result of legislative, executive, or judicial findings of past discrimination.

WESTLAW Summary

White employee brought action against employer and union challenging legality of plan for on-the-job training which mandated a one-for-one quota for minority workers admitted to the program. The United States District Court for the Eastern District of Louisiana enjoined operation of the agreement, and employer and union appealed. The Court of Appeals affirmed, and certiorari was granted. The Supreme Court held that: (1) Title VII's prohibitions against racial discrimination does not condemn all private, voluntary, race-conscious affirmative action plans, and (2) an affirmative action plan that was collectively bargained by an employer and a union and that reserved for black employees 50 percent of the openings in an in-plant craft training program until the percentage of black craft workers in plant was commensurate with the percentage of blacks in the local labor force did not violate Title VII's prohibition against racial discrimination; the purposes of the plan mirrored those of the statute, the plan did not unnecessarily trammel the interests of white employees, and the plan was a temporary measure, not intended to maintain racial balance, but simply to eliminate a manifest racial imbalance.

Case Excerpts

Mr. Justice BRENNAN delivered the opinion of the Court.

Challenged here is the legality of an affirmative action plan—collectively bargained by an employer and a union—that reserves for black employees 50% of the openings in an in-plant craft-training program until the percentage of black craft-workers in the plant is commensurate with the percentage of blacks in the local labor force. The question for decision is whether Congress, in Title VII of the Civil Rights Act of 1964, left employers and unions in the private sector free to take such race-conscious steps to eliminate manifest racial imbalances in traditionally segregated job categories. We hold that Title VII does not prohibit such race-conscious affirmative action plans.

In 1974, petitioner United Steelworkers of America (USWA) and petitioner Kaiser Aluminum & Chemical Corp. (Kaiser) entered into a master collective-bargaining agreement covering terms and conditions of employment at 15 Kaiser plants. The agreement contained, inter alia, an affirmative action plan designed to eliminate conspicuous racial imbalances in Kaiser's then almost exclusively white craft-work forces. Black craft-hiring goals were set for each Kaiser plant equal to the percentage of blacks in the respective local labor forces. To enable plants to meet these goals, on-the-job training programs were established to teach unskilled production workers—black and white—the skills necessary to become craftworkers. The plan reserved for black employees 50% of the openings in these newly created in-plant training programs.

(1) This case arose from the operation of the plan at Kaiser's plant in Gramercy, La. Until 1974, Kaiser hired as craftworkers for that plant only persons who had had prior craft experience. Because blacks had long been excluded from craft unions, few were able to present such cre-

dentials. As a consequence, prior to 1974 only 1.83% (5 out of 273) of the skilled craftworkers at the Gramercy plant were black, even though the work force in the Gramercy area was approximately 39% black.

Pursuant to the national agreement Kaiser altered its craft-hiring practice in the Gramercy plant. Rather than hiring already trained outsiders, Kaiser established a training program to train its production workers to fill craft openings. Selection of craft trainees was made on the basis of seniority, with the proviso that at least 50% of the new trainees were to be black until the percentage of black skilled craftworkers in the Gramercy plant approximated the percentage of blacks in the local labor force.

During 1974, the first year of the operation of the Kaiser-USWA affirmative action plan, 13 craft trainees were selected from Gramercy's production work force. Of these, seven were black and six white. The most senior black selected into the program had less seniority than several white production workers whose bids for admission were rejected. Thereafter one of those white production workers, respondent Brian Weber (hereafter respondent), instituted this class action in the United States District Court for the Eastern District of Louisiana.

* * * *

Respondent argues that Congress intended in Title VII to prohibit all race-conscious affirmative action plans. Respondent's argument rests upon a literal interpretation of sections 703(a) and (d) of the Act. Those sections make it unlawful to "discriminate . . . because of . . . race" in hiring and in the selection of apprentices for training programs. * * *

Respondent's argument is not without force. But it overlooks the significance of the fact that the Kaiser-USWA plan is an affirmative action plan voluntarily adopted by private parties to eliminate traditional patterns of racial segregation. * * * The prohibition against racial discrimination in sections 703(a) and (d) of Title VII must therefore be read against the background of the legislative history of Title VII and the historical context from which the Act arose. Examination of those sources makes clear that an interpretation of the sections that forbade all race-conscious affirmative action would "bring about an end completely at variance with the purpose of the statute" and must be rejected.

Congress' primary concern in enacting the prohibition against racial discrimination in Title VII of the Civil Rights Act of 1964 was with "the plight of the Negro in our economy." Before 1964, blacks were largely relegated to "unskilled and semi-skilled jobs." Because of automation the number of such jobs was rapidly decreasing. As a consequence, "the relative position of the Negro worker (was) steadily worsening. In 1947 the nonwhite unemployment rate was only 64 percent higher than the white rate; in 1962 it was 124 percent higher." Congress considered this a serious social problem. * * *

* * * *

Congress feared that the goals of the Civil Rights Act—the integration of blacks into the mainstream of American society—could not be achieved unless this trend were reversed. And Congress recognized that that would not be possible unless blacks were able to secure jobs "which have a future." * * *

* * * *

Given this legislative history, we cannot agree with respondent that Congress intended to prohibit the private sector from taking effective steps to accomplish the goal that Congress designed Title VII to achieve. The very statutory words intended as a spur or catalyst to cause "employers and unions to self-examine and to self-evaluate their employment practices and to endeavor to eliminate, so far as possible, the last vestiges of an unfortunate and ignominious page in this country's history," cannot be interpreted as an absolute prohibition against all private, voluntary, race-conscious affirmative action efforts to hasten the elimination of such vestiges. It would be ironic indeed if a law triggered by a Nation's concern over centuries of racial injustice and intended to improve the lot of those who had "been excluded from the American dream for so long," constituted the first legislative prohibition of all voluntary, private, race-conscious efforts to abolish traditional patterns of racial segregation and hierarchy.

Our conclusion is further reinforced by examination of the language and legislative history of section 703(j) of Title VII. Opponents of Title VII raised two related arguments against the bill. First, they argued that the Act would be interpreted to require employers with racially imbalanced work forces to grant preferential treatment to racial minorities in order to integrate. Second, they argued that employers with racially imbalanced work forces would grant preferential treatment to racial minorities, even if not required to do so by the Act. Had Congress meant to prohibit all race-conscious affirmative action, as respondent urges, it easily could have answered both objections by providing that Title VII would not require or permit racially preferential integration efforts. But Congress did not choose such a course. * * *

We therefore hold that Title VII's prohibition in sections 703(a) and (d) against racial discrimination does not condemn all private, voluntary, race-conscious affirmative action plans.

* * * *

We conclude, therefore, that the adoption of the Kaiser-USWA plan for the Gramercy plant falls within the area of discretion left by Title VII to the private sector voluntarily to adopt affirmative action plans designed to eliminate conspicuous racial imbalance in traditionally segregated job categories. * * *

Decision

Reversed.

James P. **WESBERRY**, Jr., et al.,
v.
Carl E. **SANDERS**, et al.
376 U.S. 1, 84 S.Ct. 526, 11 L.Ed.2d 481.
Argued Nov. 18 and 19, 1963.
Decided Feb. 17, 1964.

Introduction

A Fourteenth Amendment/Congressional districting case in which the Court ruled that the state of Georgia's formation of Congressional districts created such huge population differences that they violated the Constitution. This case was the basis of the Court's ruling later requiring one person, one vote.

WESTLAW Summary

Action, in the United States District Court for the Northern District of Georgia, by qualified voters to strike down a Georgia statute prescribing congressional districts. The three-judge District Court dismissed the complaint, and plaintiffs appealed. The Supreme Court held that the complaint presented a justiciable controversy, and that the apportionment of congressional districts so that single congressman represented from two to three times as many Fifth District voters as were represented by each of the congressmen from the other Georgia districts grossly discriminated against voters in the Fifth District in violation of the constitutional requirement that representatives be chosen by people of the several states.

Case Excerpts

Mr. Justice BLACK delivered the opinion of the Court.

Appellants are citizens and qualified voters of Fulton County, Georgia, and as such are entitled to vote in congressional elections in

Georgia's Fifth Congressional District. That district, one of ten created by a 1931 Georgia statute, includes Fulton, DeKalb, and Rockdale Counties and has a population according to the 1960 census of 823,680. The average population of the ten districts is 394,312, less than half that of the Fifth. One district, the Ninth, has only 272,154 people, less than one-third as many as the Fifth. Since there is only one Congressman for each district, this inequality of population means that the Fifth District's Congressman has to represent from two to three times as many people as do Congressmen from some of the other Georgia districts.

Claiming that these population disparities deprived them and voters similarly situated of a right under the Federal Constitution to have their votes for Congressmen given the same weight as the votes of other Georgians, the appellants brought this action asking that the Georgia statute be declared invalid and that the appellees, the Governor and Secretary of State of Georgia, be enjoined from conducting elections under it. * * *

* * * We agree with the District Court that the 1931 Georgia apportionment grossly discriminates against voters in the Fifth Congressional District. A single Congressman represents from two to three times as many Fifth District voters as are represented by each of the Congressmen from the other Georgia congressional districts. The apportionment statute thus contracts the value of some votes and expands that of others. If the Federal Constitution intends that when qualified voters elect members of Congress each vote be given as much weight as any other vote, then this statute cannot stand.

* * * *

It would defeat the principle solemnly embodied in the Great Compromise—equal representation in the House for equal numbers of people—for us to hold that, within the States, legislatures may draw the lines of congressional districts in such a way as to give some voters a greater voice in choosing a Congressman than others. The House of Representatives, the Convention agreed, was to represent the people as individuals, and on a basis of complete equality for each voter. * * *

* * * *

It is in the light of such history that we must construe Art[icle] I, [Section] 2, of the Constitution, which, carrying out the ideas of Madison and those of like views, provides that Representatives shall be chosen "by the People of the several States" and shall be "apportioned among the several States * * * according to their respective Numbers." It is not surprising that our Court has held that this Article gives persons qualified to vote a constitutional right to vote and to have their votes counted. No right is more precious in a free country than that of having a voice in the election of those who make the laws under which, as good citizens, we must live. Other rights, even the most basic, are illusory if the right to vote is undermined. Our Constitution leaves no room for classification of people in a way that unnecessarily abridges this right. * * *

* * * *

While it may not be possible to draw congressional districts with mathematical precision, that is no excuse for ignoring our Constitution's plain objective of making equal representation for equal numbers of people the fundamental goal for the House of Representatives. That is the high standard of justice and common sense which the Founders set for us.

Decision

Reversed and remanded.

YOUNGSTOWN SHEET & TUBE CO. et al.
v.
SAWYER.
343 U.S. 579, 72 S.Ct. 863, 96 L.Ed. 1153.
Argued May 12 and May 13, 1952.
Decided June 2, 1952.

Introduction

A case challenging the president's power to seize private industrial facilities during a national emergency. The Supreme Court held that the president had exceeded his constitutional powers when he ordered that striking steel mills be seized by the government to keep them operational during wartime.

WESTYLAW Summary

The Youngstown Sheet & Tube Company and other steel companies named in a list attached to Executive Order No. 10340, promulgated April 8, 1952, directing seizure of the plants of such companies, brought actions against Charles Sawyer, Secretary of Commerce, praying for declaratory judgments and injunctive relief. The United States District Court for the District of Columbia, David A. Pine, J., granted plaintiffs' motions for temporary injunctions. Certiorari was granted by the United States Supreme Court after the Court of Appeals for the District of Columbia Circuit had issued stay orders. Mr. Justice Black delivered the opinion of the court holding that the seizure order was not within the constitutional power of the President.

Case Excerpts

Mr. Justice BLACK delivered the opinion of the Court.

We are asked to decide whether the President was acting within his constitutional power when he issued an order directing the Secretary of Commerce to take possession of and operate most of the Nation's steel mills. The mill owners argue that the President's order amounts to lawmaking, a legislative function which the Constitution has expressly confided to the Congress and not to the President. The Government's position is that the order was made on findings of the President that his action was necessary to avert a national catastrophe which would inevitably result from a stoppage of steel production, and that in meeting this grave emergency the President was acting within the aggregate of his constitutional powers as the Nation's Chief Executive and the Commander in Chief of the Armed Forces of the United States. The issue emerges here from the following series of events:

In the latter part of 1951, a dispute arose between the steel companies and their employees over terms and conditions that should be included in new collective bargaining agreements. Long-continued conferences failed to resolve the dispute. On December 18, 1951, the employees' representative, United Steelworkers of America, C.I.O., gave notice of an intention to strike when the existing bargaining agreements expired on December 31. The Federal Mediation and Conciliation Service then intervened in an effort to get labor and management to agree. This failing, the President on December 22, 1951, referred the dispute to the Federal Wage Stabilization Board to investigate and make recommendations for fair and equitable terms of settlement. This Board's report resulted in no settlement. On April 4, 1952, the Union gave notice of a nation-wide strike called to begin at 12:01 a.m. April 9. The indispensability of steel as a component of substantially all weapons and other war materials led the President to believe that the proposed work stoppage would immediately jeopardize our national defense and that governmental seizure of the steel mills was necessary in order to assure the continued availability of steel. Reciting these considerations for his action, the President, a few hours before the strike was to begin, issued Executive Order 10340 * * *. The order directed the Secretary of Commerce to take possession of most of the steel mills and keep them running. The Secretary immediately issued his own possessory orders, calling upon the presidents of the various seized companies to serve as operating managers for the United States. They were directed to carry on their activities in accordance with regulations and directions of the

Secretary. The next morning the President sent a message to Congress reporting his action. Twelve days later he sent a second message. Congress has taken no action.

Obeying the Secretary's orders under protest, the companies brought proceedings against him in the District Court. Their complaints charged that the seizure was not authorized by an act of Congress or by any constitutional provisions. The District Court was asked to declare the orders of the President and the Secretary invalid and to issue preliminary and permanent injunctions restraining their enforcement. Opposing the motion for preliminary injunction, the United States asserted that a strike disrupting steel production for even a brief period would so endanger the well-being and safety of the Nation that the President had "inherent power" to do what he had done—power "supported by the Constitution, by historical precedent, and by court decisions." The Government also contended that in any event no preliminary injunction should be issued because the companies had made no showing that their available legal remedies were inadequate or that their injuries from seizure would be irreparable. Holding against the Government on all points, the District Court on April 30 issued a preliminary injunction restraining the Secretary from "continuing the seizure and possession of the plant * * * and from acting under the purported authority of Executive Order No. 10340." On the same day the Court of Appeals stayed the District Court's injunction. Deeming it best that the issues raised be promptly decided by this Court, we granted certiorari on May 3 and set the cause for argument on May 12.

Two crucial issues have developed: First. Should final determination of the constitutional validity of the President's order be made in this case which has proceeded no further than the preliminary injunction stage? Second. If so, is the seizure order within the constitutional power of the President?

It is urged that there were nonconstitutional grounds upon which the District Court could have denied the preliminary injunction and thus have followed the customary judicial practice of declining to reach and decide constitutional questions until compelled to do so. On this basis it is argued that equity's extraordinary injunctive relief should have been denied because (a) seizure of the companies' properties did not inflict irreparable damages, and (b) there were available legal remedies adequate to afford compensation for any possible damages which they might suffer. While separately argued by the Government, these two contentions are here closely related, if not identical. Arguments as to both rest in large part on the Government's claim that should the seizure ultimately be held unlawful, the companies could recover full compensation in the Court of Claims for the unlawful taking. Prior cases in this Court have cast doubt on the right to recover in the Court of Claims on account of properties unlawfully taken by government officials for public use as these properties were alleged to have been. Moreover, seizure and governmental operation of these going businesses were bound to result in many present and future damages of such nature as to be difficult, if not incapable, of measurement. Viewing the case this way, and in the light of the facts presented, the District Court saw no reason for delaying decision of the constitutional validity of the orders. We agree with the District Court and can see no reason why that question was not ripe for determination on the record presented. We shall therefore consider and determine that question now.

The President's power, if any, to issue the order must stem either from an act of Congress or from the Constitution itself. There is no statute that expressly authorizes the President to take possession of property as he did here. Nor is there any act of Congress to which our attention has been directed from which such a power can fairly be implied. Indeed, we do not understand the Government to rely on statutory authorization for this seizure. There are two statutes which do authorize the President to take both personal and real property under certain conditions. However, the Government admits that these conditions were not met and that the President's order was not rooted in either of the statutes. The Government refers to the seizure provisions of one of these statutes ([Section] 201(b) of the Defense Production Act) as "much too cumbersome, involved, and time-consuming for the crisis which was at hand."

Moreover, the use of the seizure technique to solve labor disputes in order to prevent work stoppages was not only unauthorized by any congressional enactment; prior to this controversy, Congress had refused to adopt that method of settling labor disputes. When the Taft-Hartley Act was under consideration in 1947, Congress rejected an amendment which would have authorized such governmental seizures in cases of emergency. Apparently it was thought that the technique of seizure, like that of compulsory arbitration, would interfere with the process of collective bargaining. Consequently, the plan Congress adopted in that Act did not provide for seizure under any circumstances. Instead, the plan sought to bring about settlements by use of the customary devices of mediation, conciliation, investigation by boards of inquiry, and public reports. In some instances temporary injunctions were authorized to provide cooling-off periods. All this failing, unions were left free to strike after a secret vote by employees as to whether they wished to accept their employers' final settlement offer.

It is clear that if the President had authority to issue the order he did, it must be found in some provisions of the Constitution. And it is not claimed that express constitutional language grants this power to the President. The contention is that presidential power should be implied from the aggregate of his powers under the Constitution. Particular reliance is placed on provisions in Article II which say that "the executive Power shall be vested in a President * * * "; that "he shall take Care that the Laws be faithfully executed"; and that he "shall be Commander in Chief of the Army and Navy of the United States."

The order cannot properly be sustained as an exercise of the President's military power as Commander in Chief of the Armed Forces. * * *

Nor can the seizure order be sustained because of the several constitutional provisions that grant executive power to the President. In the framework of our Constitution, the President's power to see that the laws are faithfully executed refutes the idea that he is to be a lawmaker. The Constitution limits his functions in the lawmaking process to the recommending of laws he thinks wise and the vetoing of laws he thinks bad. And the Constitution is neither silent nor equivocal about who shall make laws which the President is to execute. The first section of the first article says that "All legislative Powers herein granted shall be vested in a Congress of the United States * * *." * * *

The President's order does not direct that a congressional policy be executed in a manner prescribed by Congress—it directs that a presidential policy be executed in a manner prescribed by the President. The preamble of the order itself, like that of many statutes, sets out reasons why the President believes certain policies should be adopted, proclaims these policies as rules of conduct to be followed, and again, like a statute, authorizes a government official to promulgate additional rules and regulations consistent with the policy proclaimed and needed to carry that policy into execution. The power of Congress to adopt such public policies as those proclaimed by the order is beyond question. It can authorize the taking of private property for public use. It can makes laws regulating the relationships between employers and employees, prescribing rules designed to settle labor disputes, and fixing wages and working conditions in certain fields of our economy. The Constitution did not subject this law-making power of Congress to presidential or military supervision or control.

It is said that other Presidents without congressional authority have taken possession of private business enterprises in order to settle labor disputes. But even if this be true, Congress has not thereby lost its exclusive constitutional authority to make laws necessary and proper to carry out the powers vested by the Constitution "in the Government of the United States, or in any Department or Officer thereof."

The Founders of this Nation entrusted the law making power to the Congress alone in both good and bad times. It would do no good to recall the historical events, the fears of power and the hopes for freedom that lay behind their choice. Such a review would but confirm our holding that this seizure order cannot stand.

Decision

The judgment of the District Court is affirmed.

James **ZURCHER**, etc., et al., Petitioners,
v.
The **STANFORD DAILY** et al.
436 U.S. 547, 98 S.Ct. 1970, 56 L.Ed.2d 525.
Argued Jan. 17, 1978.
Decided May 31, 1978.
Rehearing Denied Oct. 2, 1978.

Introduction

A Fourth Amendment case in which the Supreme Court held that a warrant to search the premises of (a campus newspaper office) for evidence relating to criminal activity did not violate the Fourth Amendment, which prohibits unreasonable searches and seizures.

WESTLAW Summary

University student newspaper and various staff members brought civil rights actions seeking declaratory and injunctive relief against, among others, police officers who conducted search of newspaper premises for negatives, films and pictures revealing identities of demonstrators who assaulted police officers during confrontation involving seizure of administrative offices of university hospital. The United States District Court for the Northern District of California, granted declaratory relief. The Court of Appeals affirmed. Writs of certiorari were granted. The Supreme Court, Mr. Justice White, held that: (1) Fourth Amendment does not prevent a state from issuing a warrant to search for evidence simply because the owner or possessor of the place to be searched is not reasonably suspected of criminal involvement and, hence, in such third-party search situations the government is not limited to use of a subpoena duces tecum, and (2) properly administered, preconditions for search warrant, which conditions must be applied with particular exactitude when First Amendment interests would be endangered, constitute adequate safeguards against interference with the press' ability to gather, analyze and disseminate news.

Case Excerpts

Mr. Justice WHITE delivered the opinion of the Court.

The terms of the Fourth Amendment, applicable to the States by virtue of the Fourteenth Amendment, are familiar: "The right of the people to be secure in their persons, houses, papers, and effects, against unreasonable searches and seizures, shall not be violated, and no Warrants shall issue, but upon probable cause, supported by Oath or affirmation, and particularly describing the place to be searched, and the persons or things to be seized." As heretofore understood, the Amendment has not been a barrier to warrants to search property on which there is probable cause to believe that fruits, instrumentalities, or evidence of crime is located, whether or not the owner or possessor of the premises to be searched is himself reasonably suspected of complicity in the crime being investigated. We are now asked to reconstrue the Fourth Amendment and to hold for the first time that when the place to be searched is occupied by a person not then a suspect, a warrant to search for criminal objects and evidence reasonably believed to be located there should not issue except in the most unusual circumstances, and that except in such circumstances, a subpoena duces tecum must be relied upon to recover the objects or evidence sought.

Late in the day on Friday, April 9, 1971, officers of the Palo Alto Police Department and of the Santa Clara County Sheriff's Department responded to a call from the director of the Stanford University Hospital requesting the removal of a large group of demonstrators who had seized the hospital's administrative offices and occupied them since the previous afternoon. After several futile efforts to persuade the demonstrators to leave peacefully, more drastic measures were employed. The demonstrators had barricaded the doors at both ends of a hall adjacent to the administrative offices. The police chose to force their way in at the west end of the corridor. As they did so, a group of demonstrators emerged through the doors at the east end and, armed with sticks and clubs, attacked the group of nine police officers stationed there. One officer was knocked to the floor and struck repeatedly on the head; another suffered a broken shoulder. All nine were injured. There were no police photographers at the east doors, and most bystanders and reporters were on the west side. The officers themselves were able to identify only two of their assailants, but one of them did see at least one person photographing the assault at the east doors.

On Sunday, April 11, a special edition of the Stanford Daily (Daily), a student newspaper published at Stanford University, carried articles and photographs devoted to the hospital protest and the violent clash between demonstrators and police. The photographs carried the byline of a Daily staff member and indicated that he had been at the east end of the hospital hallway where he could have photographed the assault on the nine officers. The next day, the Santa Clara County District Attorney's Office secured a warrant from the Municipal Court for an immediate search of the Daily's offices for negatives, film, and pictures showing the events and occurrences at the hospital on the evening of April 9. The warrant issued on a finding of "just, probable and reasonable cause for believing that: Negatives and photographs and films, evidence material and relevant to the identity of the perpetrators of felonies, to wit, Battery on a Peace Officer, and Assault with Deadly Weapon, will be located [on the premises of the Daily]." The warrant affidavit contained no allegation or indication that members of the Daily staff were in any way involved in unlawful acts at the hospital.

The search pursuant to the warrant was conducted later that day by four police officers and took place in the presence of some members of the Daily staff. The Daily's photographic laboratories, filing cabinets, desks, and wastepaper baskets were searched. Locked drawers and rooms were not opened. The officers apparently had opportunity to read notes and correspondence during the search; but, contrary to claims of the staff, the officers denied that they had exceeded the limits of the warrant. They had not been advised by the staff that the areas they were searching contained confidential materials. The search revealed only the photographs that had already been published on April 11, and no materials were removed from the Daily's office.

A month later the Daily and various members of its staff, respondents here, brought a civil action in the United States District Court for the Northern District of California seeking declaratory and injunctive relief under 42 U.S.C. [Section] 1983 against the police officers who conducted the search, the chief of police, the district attorney and one of his deputies, and the judge who had issued the warrant. The complaint alleged that the search of the Daily's office had deprived respondents under color of state law of rights secured to them by the First, Fourth, and Fourteenth Amendments of the United States Constitution.

The District Court denied the request for an injunction but, on respondents' motion for summary judgment, granted declaratory relief. The court did not question the existence of probable cause to believe that a crime had been committed and to believe that relevant evidence would be found on the Daily's premises. It held, however, that the Fourth and Fourteenth Amendments forbade the issuance of a warrant to search for materials in possession of one not suspected of crime unless there is probable cause to believe, based on facts presented in a sworn affidavit, that a subpoena duces tecum would be impracticable. Moreover, the failure to honor a subpoena would not alone justify a warrant; it must also appear that the possessor of the objects sought would disregard a court order not to remove or destroy them. The District Court further held that where the innocent object of the search is a newspaper, First Amendment interests are also involved and that such a search is constitutionally permissible "only in the rare circumstance where there is a clear showing that (1) important materials will be destroyed or removed from the jurisdiction; and (2) a restraining order would be futile." Since these preconditions to a valid warrant had not been satisfied here, the search of the Daily's offices was declared to have been illegal. The Court of Appeals affirmed per curiam, adopting the opinion of the District Court. We issued the writs of certiorari requested by petitioners.

The issue here is how the Fourth Amendment is to be construed and applied to the "third party" search, the recurring situation where state authorities have probable cause to believe that fruits, instrumentalities, or other evidence of crime is located on identified property but do not then have probable cause to believe that the owner or possessor of the property is himself implicated in the crime that has occurred or is occurring. Because under the District Court's rule impracticability can be shown only by furnishing facts demonstrating that the third party will not only disobey the subpoena but also ignore a restraining order not to move or destroy the property, it is apparent that only in unusual situations could the State satisfy such a severe burden and that for all practical purposes the effect of the rule is that fruits, instrumentalities, and evidence of crime may be recovered from third parties only by subpoena, not by search warrant. At least, we assume that the District Court did not intend its rule to be toothless and anticipated that only subpoenas would be available in many cases where without the rule a search warrant would issue.

It is an understatement to say that there is no direct authority in this or any other federal court for the District Court's sweeping revision of the Fourth Amendment. Under existing law, valid warrants may be issued to search any property, whether or not occupied by a third party, at which there is probable cause to believe that fruits, instrumentalities, or evidence of a crime will be found. Nothing on the face of the Amendment suggests that a third-party search warrant should not normally issue. The Warrant Clause speaks of search warrants issued on "probable cause" and "particularly describing the place to be searched, and the persons or things to be seized." In situations where the State does not seek to seize "persons" but only those "things" which there is probable cause to believe are located on the place to be searched, there is no apparent basis in the language of the Amendment for also imposing the requirements for a valid arrest—probable cause to believe that the third party is implicated in the crime.

* * * *

The critical element in a reasonable search is not that the owner of the property is suspected of crime but that there is reasonable cause to believe that the specific "things" to be searched for and seized are located on the property to which entry is sought. * * *

* * * *

* * * As we understand the structure and language of the Fourth Amendment and our cases expounding it, valid warrants to search property may be issued when it is satisfactorily demonstrated to the magistrate that fruits, instrumentalities, or evidence of crime is located on the premises. The Fourth Amendment has itself struck the balance between privacy and public need, and there is no occasion or justification for a court to revise the Amendment and strike a new balance by denying the search warrant in the circumstances present here and by insisting that the investigation proceed by subpoena duces tecum, whether on the theory that the latter is a less intrusive alternative or otherwise.

This is not to question that "reasonableness" is the overriding test of compliance with the Fourth Amendment or to assert that searches, however or whenever executed, may never be unreasonable if supported by a warrant issued on probable cause and properly identifying the place to be searched and the property to be seized. We do hold, however, that the courts may not, in the name of Fourth Amendment reasonableness, prohibit the States from issuing warrants to search for evidence simply because the owner or possessor of the place to be searched is not then reasonably suspected of criminal involvement.

In any event, the reasons presented by the District Court and adopted by the Court of Appeals for arriving at its remarkable conclusion do not withstand analysis. First, as we have said, it is apparent that whether the third-party occupant is suspect or not, the State's interest in enforcing the criminal law and recovering the evidence remains the same; and it is the seeming innocence of the property owner that the District Court relied on to foreclose the warrant to search. But, as respondents themselves now concede, if the third party knows that contraband or other illegal materials are on his property, he is sufficiently culpable to justify the issuance of a search warrant. * * *

Second, we are unpersuaded that the District Court's new rule denying search warrants against third parties and insisting on subpoenas would substantially further privacy interests without seriously undermining law enforcement efforts. Because of the fundamental public interest in implementing the criminal law, the search warrant, a heretofore effective and constitutionally acceptable enforcement tool, should not be suppressed on the basis of surmise and without solid evidence supporting the change. * * *

* * * *

The District Court held, and respondents assert here, that whatever may be true of third-party searches generally, where the third party is a newspaper, there are additional factors derived from the First Amendment that justify a nearly per se rule forbidding the search warrant and permitting only the subpoena duces tecum. The general submission is that searches of newspaper offices for evidence of crime reasonably believed to be on the premises will seriously threaten the ability of the press to gather, analyze, and disseminate news. This is said to be true for several reasons: First, searches will be physically disruptive to such an extent that timely publication will be impeded. Second, confidential sources of information will dry up, and the press will also lose opportunities to cover various events because of fears of the participants that press files will be readily available to the authorities. Third, reporters will be deterred from recording and preserving their recollections for future use if such information is subject to seizure. Fourth, the processing of news and its dissemination will be chilled by the prospects that searches will disclose internal editorial deliberations. Fifth, the press will resort to self-censorship to conceal its possession of information of potential interest to the police.

* * * It is true that the struggle from which the Fourth Amendment emerged "is largely a history of conflict between the Crown and the press" and that in issuing warrants and determining the reasonableness of a search, state and federal magistrates should be aware that "unrestricted power of search and seizure could also be an instrument for stifling liberty of expression." * * *

Neither the Fourth Amendment nor the cases requiring consideration of First Amendment values in issuing search warrants, however, call for imposing the regime ordered by the District Court. Aware of the long struggle between Crown and press and desiring to curb unjustified official intrusions, the Framers took the enormously important step of subjecting searches to the test of reasonableness and to the general rule requiring search warrants issued by neutral magistrates. They nevertheless did not forbid warrants where the press was involved, did not require special showings that subpoenas would be impractical , and did not insist that the owner of the place to be searched, if connected with the press, must be shown to be implicated in the offense being investigated. Further, the prior cases do no more than insist that the courts apply the warrant requirements with particular exactitude when First Amendment interests would be endangered by the search. As we see it, no more than this is required where the warrant requested is for the seizure of criminal evidence reasonably believed to be on the premises occupied by a newspaper. Properly administered, the preconditions for a warrant—probable cause, specificity with respect to the place to be searched and the things to be seized, and overall reasonableness—should afford sufficient protection against the harms that are assertedly threatened by warrants for searching newspaper offices.

* * * *

We accordingly reject the reasons given by the District Court and adopted by the Court of Appeals for holding the search for photographs at the Stanford Daily to have been unreasonable within the meaning of the Fourth Amendment and in violation of the First Amendment. Nor has anything else presented here persuaded us that the Amendments forbade this search.

Decision

It follows that the judgment of the Court of Appeals is reversed. So ordered.

Notes

Notes

Notes

Notes

Notes

Notes

Notes

Notes